HEALING ⟍ES

OTHER BOOKS

by Robert Leichtman, M.D. & Carl Japikse

Active Meditation: The Western Tradition
Forces of the Zodiac
The Art of Living (five volumes)
The Life of Spirit (five volumes)

by Robert Leichtman, M.D.

From Heaven to Earth (24 books)

by Carl Japikse

The Light Within Us
The Hour Glass

HEALING LINES

A New Interpretation
of the I Ching
For Healing Inquiries

By Robert R. Leichtman, M.D.
and Carl Japikse

ARIEL PRESS
Columbus, Ohio

No royalties are paid on this book

This book is published in honor
of the service given to Light
by Lee Myers

HEALING LINES
Copyright © 1989 by Light

All Rights Reserved. No part of this book may be used or
reproduced in any manner whatsoever without written
permission, except in the case of brief quotations embodied
in articles and reviews. Printed in the United States of
America. Direct inquiries to: Ariel Press, P.O. Box 249,
Canal Winchester, Ohio 43110.

ISBN 0-89804-090-6

The I Ching

The I Ching is one of the best systems of "practical philosophy" ever devised. Philosophy is meant to be the pursuit of truth and wisdom. The word itself means "the love of knowledge." But modern philosophy has lost track of its roots. Too often, the pursuit of truth has been replaced by a debate of ideas. Debates can be fascinating, of course, but they tend to polarize thinking, not unite it. As a result, modern philosophy has become fragmented and disconnected, leading to such aberrations of thought as existentialism.

Worst of all, the study of philosophy has become so specialized that it no longer speaks to the average person, even the well-educated average person. It has become impractical. The great ideas of philosophy no longer shape daily thinking and behavior as they once did. Philosophy has become abstruse and esoteric, the plaything of theorists living in the proverbial ivory tower.

This is not what philosophy is meant to be. It is meant to be a practical source of values, mental principles, and guidance upon which intelligent people can base their thinking. It should be accessible at least to the educated, if not to every man and woman in the market place. Ideally, it should be a body of ideas that can be easily consulted and relied upon for a determinination of basic values, self-examination, and all types of decision making.

It is interesting that the I Ching has been gaining popularity in the West at the same time that our own philosophical systems are becoming more and more arcane. The average intelligent person senses a need for a practical philosophical system, even if the academics and intellectuals do not. And so an increasing number of people are turning to the I Ching, and discovering that it embodies a great deal of truth and insight that can be easily tapped.

The I Ching is a "practical" system because it can be consulted for practical insight and solutions into the ordinary problems of daily living—business decisions, health problems, the challenge of raising children, and so on. Those who do not understand the I Ching sometimes think of it as a system of fortune telling, but it is not. It is a philosophical system that has been developed by some of the greatest minds China has produced. The fact that it can be used by people of average intelligence to help make sense of their lives, as well as the highly educated, only serves to broaden its value, not diminish it.

The Chinese have worked with the I Ching for thousands of years. In the West, we have worked with it for about fifty years, and only intensely for half of that time. It was Carl Jung's work with the I Ching, more than anything else, that brought this remarkable system to the attention of a large number of people.

Because of the relatively short time we have worked with this system, most people still find it somewhat puzzling to use at times. This is because the commentaries on the I Ching have all been translations of the original Chinese texts, written by Chinese philosophers using the Chinese language and Chinese thought patterns to communicate with Chinese. This is perfectly normal. But a Westerner wanting insight into his or her arthritis may find it a little daunting to try to understand what the I Ching is answering, if using one of the standard texts.

Recognizing this problem, we decided it was time to do something to correct it. In specific, we saw the enormous potential of using the modern computer to help make the ancient guidance of the I Ching even more practical for the Western mind.

The object was not just to program the computer to construct the hexagrams by random process; after all, this is something that can be done just as easily with three coins! The purpose of computerizing the I Ching was to create a series of modules that could be rapidly accessed by the computer, depending upon the kind of question the user wished to ask. In this way, the commentary of each hexagram could be specifically tailored to the kind of inquiry being made.

In other words, if the user wished to ask a question about health, he or she would direct the computer to select the health module. If the question pertained to business, the user would select the business decision module on the computer's menu. The question would then be typed in, the hexagram generated by random selection, and the appropriate commentary would appear.

All that remained to be done was develop a

computer program—and to write the text for several different modules!

The computer program, *I Ching On Line,* was developed by James D. Davis, Ph.D., a retired professor of mathematics from Fairleigh Dickinson University.

This book is the text of the first module developed. It deals exclusively with health and healing issues.

In writing the text, we have avoided making a direct translation. Instead, we intuitively "dissected" each hexagram and examined it in its original, archetypal form, then restated these basic ideas so that they apply directly to questions about health and healing, in terms that can be understood by modern Westerners.

The same approach will be adopted in preparing the text for subsequent modules, which will deal with "making decisions," "relationships" and "personal growth." Our goal is to help make the I Ching the tool of practical philosophy it has always been meant to be.

We make no apologies for clarity and the specific focus we have given the text. We are fully aware that many specialists in the I Ching feel that its great strength is its vagueness, which forces the user to utilize his or her intuition. But truth and wisdom are never vague or confusing. They are always simple, clear, and insightful. It is usually a sign of intellectual laziness to fail to make the attempt to communicate this simplicity, clarity, and vision to others in easily understood terms.

Ideally, the text that follows is meant to be used

as an adjunct to *I Ching On Line.* Nevertheless, we also know that many people as yet do not own a personal computer, or perhaps do not have a model which will run the program. These people can still use the healing module—and the others that will follow—by using the commentary in this book (and the others that will follow) to interpret the hexagrams they generate by more traditional methods.

Our work is done. Now yours begins. The I Ching can become a source of practical philosophy for you only if you use it for that purpose. If you ask the I Ching silly, irreverent questions, it will give you flippant answers. If you try to use it as a crutch or a scapegoat, it will in essence tell you to stop using it until you are more honest in your pursuit of knowledge. But if you use it sincerely, to try to make sense out of the difficult and confusing issues of life, you will discover a source of unlimited guidance and understanding.

The I Ching is meant to be used. Use it wisely, and in good health!

How The I Ching Works

The I Ching is a system of archetypal forces, based on the principles of duality and the constancy of change. In China, the component forces of this duality are *yin* and *yang.* In English, we might call them positive and negative, male and female, or point and counterpoint.

The philosophers of ancient China observed that duality and change do not occur capriciously. The phenomena of life arise from a dynamic interaction of dualities. For this reason, there cannot be growth without resistance—or opportunity without hardship, success without failure.

To put this principle in terms of change, as one situation improves, another will decline. As one issue evolves, a second will decay. As the life of one movement grows in vitality, a competitive movement will lose momentum. As the level of competence in one group rises, it sinks in another.

The principle of duality governs all movements in life. And as these dual forces interact with one another, they generate complex change.

Since the Chinese language is based on pictographs, rather than letters, it was natural for the philosophers to translate this idea into images. But these are very abstract images, as befits the basic concept of duality. The symbol for active force was a single straight line; the symbol for passive force was a broken line.

THE EIGHT TRIGRAMS

Heaven

Lake

Fire

Thunder

Wind

Water

Mountain

Earth

The first combination of these solid and broken lines was to form a set of eight trigrams, each containing three lines. These eight trigrams are illustrated on the previous page. To these trigrams, philosophers began attaching meanings and interpretations, just as the ancient astrologers ascribed meanings to the constellations in the sky. And so, the trigram Heaven took on the meaning of raw creative energy and universal purpose. The trigram Fire, by contrast, took on the meaning of awareness—the fiery mind and brilliance.

Eventually, these trigrams were put together, one on top of the other, to form hexagrams. The upper trigram came to represent the larger picture of any situation—the view from heaven, as it were. The lower trigram came to represent the individualized focus of our daily problems.

There are a total of sixty-four hexagrams, but sixty-four is not the important number. Two is. Each hexagram is the direct result of duality and change, because each hexagram is composed of six lines, each of which is either solid or broken. Positive or negative. Active or passive.

As the system evolved, the ancient Chinese philosophers realized that few situations in life remain stagnant for very long. The hexagrams are not just abstract images—they are symbols for dynamic, active forces. And so every hexagram has the potential to change into any one of the other sixty-three, or remain static. The first hexagram represents the basic definition of a situation, as it exists now. The second indicates what the inherent energies of the situation are leading to.

It is this capacity to represent moving, living forces that make the I Ching ("I Ching" means "Book of Change") such a valuable tool of practical philosophy. Each hexagram is linked with a specific archetypal force affecting human life. As we use the I Ching to understand our problems and challenges, we begin to perceive what dynamic forces are active in our life, and where they are leading us. Patterns emerge, leading to insight.

Using the I Ching is very simple. If you have a computer and *I Ching On Line,* just call up the program, type in your question, and follow the directions to generate the hexagrams. [For more detailed help, refer to the instructions which come with the program.]

If you do not have a computer, you can generate the hexagrams by using three coins. Having thought of your question (it is best to write it down), you construct the hexagrams by tossing the coins six times. Each time you toss the three coins, there are four possible ways they can land:

• All three coins can be heads. This represents a broken line, changing. [— — •]

• All three coins can be tails. This represents a solid line, changing. [——— •]

• Two coins can be heads and one a tail. This represents an unchanging solid line. [— —]

• Two coins can be tails and one a head. This represents an unchanging broken line. [———]

The Chinese work from the bottom up. Therefore, the first toss generates the bottom line of the hexagram. The second toss generates the line above it, and so on, until all six lines are deter-

13

mined, from bottom to top.

It is helpful to develop some kind of annotation indicating changing lines. This can be a dot (•) to the right of the line or, as we use in the computer program, a triangle (Δ). The changing lines enable you to construct the second hexagram, or resolution. All unchanging lines in the first hexagram remain the same in the second hexagram. But a solid line that is changing in the first hexagram becomes a broken line in the second, and a broken line that is changing becomes a solid line. These changing lines indicate the principle of duality in action, moving from pole to pole.

In other words, hexagram #28, Point of Tension is composed of a broken, four solid, and a broken line, reading from the bottom up. If lines 2 and 3 are changing, then they create a completely different hexagram, #45, Harmony, which is composed of three broken, two solid, and a broken lines, from the bottom up.

28　　→　　45

The first hexagram defines the issue at hand. Each changing line reveals the subtle energies influencing conditions. The second hexagram indicates how the situation will be resolved.

If there are no changing lines in the first hexagram, then the situation is considered static. A second hexagram is not constructed.

In advanced uses of the I Ching, a third hexagram is generated as well. This is called the *nuclear* hexagram. It is derived by taking the second, third, and fourth lines (from the bottom up) of the first hexagram and transliterating them as the first, second, and third lines of the nuclear hexagram. The third, fourth, and fifth lines of the original hexagram are then transliterated as the fourth, fifth, and sixth lines of the nuclear.

There are only sixteen hexagrams which serve as nuclear hexagrams, each one being produced by four different hexagrams. These are obviously the most potent hexagrams of the sixty-four, representing primary archetypal forces. In general, the nuclear hexagram indicates the ideal methodology to use in handling the situation at hand.

Once these three hexagrams are generated, the process of interpretation can begin. If aided by *I Ching On Line*, the appropriate commentary will flash on the screen with just a touch of the return key. But even without a computer, the process of interpretation is still relatively easy.

Determine the number of each of the three hexagrams. Then, starting with the first hexagram, turn to the appropriate page in this book and read the commentary on the left hand page. This commentary is broken into three sections. The first is a general, overall statement about how this particular energy affects health. The second is a short description of how this energy impacts on physical health. The third section describes the effect of the energy on psychological well-being.

Read these comments carefully and reflect on them. It is often wise to reread the text several times, to make sure you fully understand it.

Next, read whatever text on the right hand page corresponds to the changing lines that apply to your consultation. In other words, if lines 2 and 3 are changing, read only the text for lines 2 and 3. Discount the rest. Should there be no changing lines, read only the text entitled "Unchanging."

Once you have fully digested the commentary for the first hexagram and its changing lines, turn to the pages which comment on the second hexagram, the Resolution. Read the text on the left hand side of the double page, but do not read any of the changing lines.

Finally, consult the text for the nuclear hexagram, again reading only the text on the left-hand side of the double page.

If you are serious about understanding more about yourself and life in general, it would be a good idea to keep a record of your I Ching consultations. Write down your question, draw or list the hexagrams that are generated, and then make notes about the insights and conclusions you derive from reading the text. Date each entry, so you can refer back to it easily at a later time.

Of course, if you are using *I Ching On Line,* the computer does all this record keeping for you.

Formulating Questions

Because of the unique module feature of *I Ching On Line*, it is usually relatively easy to interpret the resulting answers. The text is written on the assumption that the user is asking a question pertaining to psychological or physical health. In fact, the assumption is also made that the user is concerned about some facet of his or her health—in most cases, something is actively wrong or out of balance. As long as the question fits these parameters, as most will, the answers provided by the text in *Healing Lines* should be relatively straightforward.

This is not to say that this text cannot be used for questions that do not strictly fit this pattern. Like any good system of divination, this text can be used to answer any legitimate question. But the farther afield the question wanders from the focus of the module, the more intuitive interpretation will be required to arrive at the truth.

In other words, you can ask a question such as: "How can I improve the health of my relationship with so-and-so?" and get an answer. But do not expect this text to give you a literal answer. You will have to read between the lines to some extent, because you are stretching the application of the module to a degree. It would be much better to obtain the module on relationships, when it is available, and use it for this type of question.

The art of using the I Ching, in other words, lies not so much in interpreting the answers as it does in asking intelligent questions. If you can formulate your question properly, the text in *Healing Lines* will deliver the answer clearly, concisely, and fully, time after time.

It is therefore important to take whatever amount of time is necessary to formulate an intelligent, penetrating question. Do not rush through this preliminary stage. Think carefully. Reflect on your situation. What do you need to know?

Some people do not use questions. They assume that the I Ching knows better than they do what they need to hear, so they simply toss the coins without troubling themselves with a question.

This is not desirable. The I Ching does know what you need to hear, but it is incapable of communicating it to you unless you create a strong invocation for the answer. This invocation is created by focusing a potent need to know. The more intelligently and precisely you formulate your question, the better the results will be.

Most of your questions will be about yourself or close friends or loved ones, dealing with specific illnesses. There are several basic kinds of questions that can be asked.
• The first explores the origins of the illness:
What is the origin of my cancer of the liver?
What are the roots of my arthritis?
What are the inner dimensions of Dick's alcoholism?
What are the hidden aspects of Julie's mental difficulties?

- The second kind of question explores what you, or the affected person, need to be doing:

How can I best overcome my tendency toward depression?

What does Wayne need to do to correct his high blood pressure?

What changes must I make in my lifestyle to control my diabetes?

What can I do to increase immunity toward poison ivy?

- A third type of question examines what friends can do to help an ill person:

How can we best help Fred recover from his bout with pneumonia?

What's the best way to help our son get off of drugs?

How can we help Grandmother die serenely?

- It is also possible to ask questions which are less specifically focused:

What do I need to know about my health at this point in time?

What major health issues need I focus on for the next six months?

What unseen problems may be developing at inner levels of my being that have not yet manifested in physical symptoms?

What can be done to arrest the development of these unhealthy trends, and restore inner health?

It is not necessary to limit your inquiries just to personal problems. *Healing Lines* can be used to gain insight into health problems affecting all of humanity—and society. And so, you can ask questions such as:

19

What are the inner roots of AIDS?

What can be done to help patients with Alzheimer's disease?

What makes a person vulnerable to the common cold?

What is the best way for an individual to preserve good health?

What is the best way to gain relief from headaches?

What is the best way to heal a poor self-image?

What are the inner dynamics of accidents?

What is the best way for a group to heal its "poverty consciousness"?

Just about any question pertaining to health is fine, so long as it does not require a "yes" or "no" answer. The I Ching is not especially suited to yes or no questions; its purpose is to provide insight and understanding.

It is important, however, to show respect for the I Ching. For this reason, do not ask the same question repeatedly, either because you did not understand the original answer or (the more common motivation) because you did not like the answer. If you are confused by an answer, it is perfectly all right to ask for a clarification—just do not ask the exact same question again.

As an example, assume you have asked: "How can I overcome my lack of emotional control?" One of the changing lines informs you: "Consciously or unconsciously, you have accepted evil influences as a normal part of your life. These must be purged before you can achieve health." If you are unsure what these evil influences are or how they are affecting you, ask a second question: "What are these evil influences and how do they aggravate my lack of emotional control?"

In fact, one question will often lead to a whole series of other questions, just as a tiny pebble thrown into the middle of a pond will produce ripple after ripple of concentric emanations. Keep alert for possible questions and pursue the implications of your query—and its answer—to the furthest extent possible.

A question about arthritis, for instance, might reveal a tendency to be excessively rigid in the way you apply rules and regulations. This might then prompt you to ask such questions as:

What other health problems might result from this kind of rigidity?

How did I develop these tendencies to be rigid?

What is the best way to reduce this inflexibility without sacrificing my values and principles?

What damage has this rigidness done to me psychologically?

What quality of consciousness do I need to cultivate in order to repair the damage done?

You might even want to use other modules to pursue the impact of rigidness on other areas of your life—for example, in your relationships with others and in your business life.

The I Ching will never tire of your questions, as long as they are valid and sincere. You are limited only by your own imagination—and your personal need to know.

A Word of Caution

The one thing you can be sure of is that the I Ching will answer your question! This is why it is important to formulate it precisely, write it down, and keep a record of it. The I Ching will not answer the question you *meant* to ask, nor the question you *should have* asked. It will answer the question you actually did ask, as you worded it.

The question you ask becomes frozen in time, once you have generated the hexagrams that answer it. You cannot go back after the fact and reword your question—or reinterpret it because a different question will seem to fit your interpretation of the answer better! It may seem unnecessary to make a point as obvious as this, but sometimes it is the most obvious aspects of life that cause us the most trouble. So it is with the I Ching. The most common cause of confusion in using this system is poor memory. People have an enormous capacity for self-deception, and this extends to asking questions of the I Ching. Once they begin reading the commentary, they often unconsciously change the question they asked—even if they have a written record of it! They alter the question in small ways so that the answer is more favorable to them—or at least less threatening.

As an example, let's say you ask the question: "What do I need to know about the cause of my ulcers?" The answer might indicate that you have been hyperreactive to the worries, fears, and impositions of friends and loved ones. That could set you off on a tangent where you start blaming your friends and loved ones for your ulcers. But your question was not: "Who should I blame for my ulcers?" It was: "What do I need to know about the cause of my ulcers?" And the answer, quite correctly, identified your excessive emotional reactiveness. To understand the answer, you need to stick to the original question—not make up a new one that fits your need for self-deception!

Obviously, it is of great importance to eliminate this kind of self-deception in using the I Ching. Make a written record of your question, and then refer back to it again and again as you read the commentary and formulate your interpretation of it. If you do not understand the question, after all, it will be impossible to understand the answer!

In using the I Ching, the keynote should always be self-examination. We are looking for new insight into our own character and health—not for new excuses, or new scapegoats, or new rationalizations. If you are prone to self-deception, the first question you need to ask the I Ching is: "How can I heal my psychological need to deceive myself?" Only when this question is fully answered, and acted upon, should you then proceed with others.

Divine Intelligence

In using the I Ching, the big question to the Westerner is always: "How does this thing work?" We have elevated skepticism to such a high level that almost everyone asks this question when first exposed to the I Ching. Curiously, it is not a common question in China. As a culture, the Chinese are not puzzled by how the I Ching works. The only thing that puzzles them is why the average Westerner makes such a big fuss about it!

They have a point. The Judeo-Christian tradition is the major moral and philosophical basis for thinking in the West, and it is very common for Westerners to profess to believe in the omnipresence, omnipotence, and omniscience of God. "Omniscience" means not only that God is all-knowing, but on a more practical level, that divine intelligence pervades everything. Whether we are at worship, in our car, at home, or at the grocery, we are surrounded and interpenetrated by divine intelligence (and love and power!) at all times.

It is odd that people will stand up in church or temple and proclaim divine omniscience, then actually believe that they leave it all behind the moment they step outside! But they do—they believe in luck, in random sequences, and in accidents, not in divine omniscience. Frankly, it's not a record that any of us should be proud of.

Divine intelligence is designed to give us the answers we seek. If we are sufficiently enlightened we should be able to discern these answers from any common phenomena of life—as Brother Lawrence did centuries ago as he watched the leaves fall from trees in autumn and came to understand God's benevolent love and protection.

Since most of us are not this enlightened, special systems have been developed over the eons to help us communicate more easily with divine intelligence. The I Ching is one of these systems. It works because divine intelligence pervades all of life and every event of life, even something as trivial as the "random" throw of three coins or the way in which you strike your computer keyboard six times in succession.

The random action of throwing the coins or striking computer keys is not what triggers the right response; it merely helps us get our own wish life and preconceived ideas out of the way, so that we do not control the process. Once we are unable to consciously influence the selection process of the hexagrams, then divine intelligence is able to take over. Time after time, the right hexagrams are generated to answer our questions.

It is for this reason that we need to take the answers the I Ching provides seriously. And we must also always keep in mind the full context of our questions and answers.

In a very real sense, our personal world is a small but complete universe which exists as a part of the larger universe of our family, our work, our community, our nation, and humanity as a whole. As we develop personal problems, we can only understand them if we are able to see them in the larger context of these bigger spheres of influence. This is true whether the problem involves health, business, relationships, or just our own ethics and inner stability.

The I Ching is designed to help us see our connections to these larger spheres. We may believe that our problem exists only within the microcosm of our private world, but in truth the solution, whatever it is, always lies in the macrocosm. Unless we can reach out to the macrocosm and discover what the solution is, it will evade us.

Divine intelligence is not just a huge cosmic brain. It is a force field of intelligence, filled with living, dynamic energies. These energies are what are known as "archetypal forces." They are the abstract forces from which everything that is has been created.

Love, wisdom, and power are the three most basic of these forces. Others include grace, joy, beauty, peace, harmony, and abundance. Whenever we have a problem, it is a sign that we lack one of these archetypal forces, or are misusing it. We will not be able to find it within our own private world, however. We must reach out to the macrocosm for it.

The I Ching is one of the great tools for guiding us to the right force and helping us connect with it. In fact, the inner structure of the I Ching makes it clear that this system was designed with just this purpose in mind. The lower trigram in each hexagram represents the microcosm—our private world and our needs. The higher trigram represents the inner dimensions of life, the view from heaven. It does not reveal our personal world, but the larger macrocosm in which we live and move and have our being.

Given this basic structure, there are many subtle clues that can help us comprehend the I Ching more completely. It is often useful, for example, to examine each trigram in a hexagram and go back to its original meanings. Hexagram #28, for example, is composed of the trigram for joy in the upper position and the trigram for gentle influences in the lower one. By seeing the component parts in this way, it is easier to understand why this particular hexagram is called "Point of Tension." The tremendous power above may overwhelm the modest capacity for self-expression below, but if we are able to stretch our skills and talents beyond their normal ability, we can likewise seize an unparalleled opportunity. It is the archetypal energies themselves that create the point of tension—but it is up to us to determine if this crisis will produce a breakthrough, or a breakdown.

This illustrates a point that needs emphasis. Being symbols of archetypal forces, no hexagram is either good or bad. They are all divine. It is up to us to determine how they will be used. If we use these forces wisely, they will be productive. If we use them selfishly, they will be restrictive. The choice is up to us. Our future lies not in the hexagrams themselves, but in our capacity to harness their potential intelligently.

Some of the titles we have chosen for the hexagrams may at times sound ominous: The Storm,

Discord, Threat, or Schism. Others may appeal to us much more: Enrichment, Abundance, and Great Promise. But these are just labels for forces which are neither positive nor negative. They are building blocks to be used creatively. A wise person will recognize as much potential for advancement in a time of Threat as in a time of Abundance, and will act accordingly.

Another key to interpreting the hexagrams is what is known as "ruling lines." A ruling line is something like the accented syllable or syllables in a word: it is the line (or sometimes two lines) that dominates all the other lines in the hexagram. In most texts, the ruling lines are indicated as part of the commentary. We have not done so in the text for *Healing Lines* or any other module, and for a very simple reason. In many consultations of the I Ching, the ruling line will not even appear. Yet if there are three changing lines, one will be dominant for that question, even if none of the changing lines happens to be the natural ruler. If a ruling line has already been picked, it does not encourage the user to try to determine the dominant line. So we have left out the ruling lines, in the hope that the more ambitious users of this text will develop the intuitive habit of determining the true ruler, question by question.

As you read the changing lines, therefore, try to weigh which one is the strongest influence on your situation. It may be perfectly obvious, or it may be very obscure. But often once you determine which line is the true ruling force, it gives you the clue you need to interpret the rest of the message. It lets you embrace the inner forces that are at work in this situation.

Ultimately, this is what the I Ching is meant to be: a barometer of the inner forces which influence us individually and collectively. Treat it with respect, but do not be in awe of it. It is a tool that intelligent people use to understand life. If at any point in your use of the I Ching you are unsure of how to proceed next, do not become flustered. Always remember that you have at your disposal one of the greatest tools of divination ever invented. Just ask the I Ching to show you what to do next—and it will!

A NUMBERED GUIDE

TO THE

SIXTY-FOUR HEXAGRAMS

OF THE I CHING

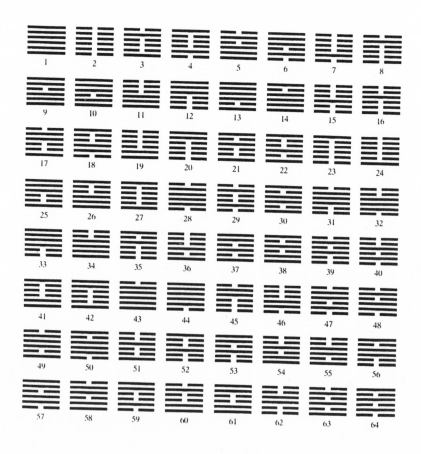

HEALING LINES

1. New Life Energy

There is an abundance of energy to be tapped at this time, as well as many opportunities to grow. It is therefore important to choose wisely and focus on primary issues at this time—to take charge of your health, to reform bad habits, and to initiate new directions in your lifestyle. Avoid distractions and trivial worries, lest you squander the energy available to you and thereby harm yourself. This new life energy is to be used to regenerate and renew health and well-being, not jeopardize it.

Physical: There is great physical vitality at hand, but you must harness it and use it wisely to promote health and well-being, not just squander it through frivolous activities or pursuits. Link activities with enlightened purpose. Visualizations and affirmations will be unusually effective.

Psychological: Enthusiasm, perhaps even euphoria, can help you harness vitality for building self-esteem, adjusting negative attitudes and moods, and recognizing opportunities. Nonetheless, you must handle these energies wisely, lest you end up a victim of over-confidence or self-deception.

THE CHANGING LINES

6: Establish a long-range plan for health, yet be mindful of your human limits. Develop your vision, but apply it with prudence and patience.

5: The effort to act in harmony with the higher self will be successful.

4: Now is the time to create an inner structure of health which will lead to a healthy lifestyle.

3: Take responsibility for your health and well-being; avoid being defensive about your problems or thinking yourself a victim.

2: Align your attitudes with the power of your ideals.

1: Avoid impulsiveness. Base actions on purpose, not raw strength.

Unchanging: There is an unusual opportunity for initiating major reform in your lifestyle, based on inner healing. If this opportunity is not seized, change for the better may become increasingly difficult.

2. Responsiveness

Your problem or illness is a natural response to some aspect of your chosen lifestyle: earlier actions, environmental pressures, or beliefs. Waste no time denying your problem; accept it as a challenge to be met and dealt with, trying to understand how it developed—and how it can be cured. The problem at hand is temporarily beyond your conscious control; the only effective way to act is through acceptance and understanding of the problem and, therefore, potentially, the solution. The best source of help is from friends and traditional sources of treatment.

Physical: This is not a problem that can be treated with an instant cure; it will have to run its natural course. You can alleviate discomfort, but must approach your illness with patience and endurance. Don't fight the illness; nurture your body's healing potential with proper diet, rest and/or exercise, and medication.

Psychological: This is not the time to be assertive, aggressive, or demand your own way. Indeed, this type of behavior may be the cause of your problem. You must learn to let others and life itself help you generate a more realistic perspective on your life. You may have overestimated the correctness and value of your beliefs and your ability to control your life.

THE CHANGING LINES

6: Learn not to struggle against forces which will only exhaust you and prevent you from pursuing your own talents and opportunities.

5: Life is not a fairy tale; you are responsible for dealing with the health problems that come to you. Avoid thinking of yourself as a victim.

4: Even illness serves a purpose; try to understand the hidden message within your problem.

3: Don't let frustration control the way in which you respond to your problem. Do not fail to do what is feasible and practical.

2: Trust your common sense and traditional methods; put more trust in practical steps toward a cure than in your personal strength and self-control.

1: The physical body is weak and vulnerable; give maximum attention to preserving and protecting your health.

Unchanging: God designed us to be well and healthy. It is our responsibility to be continually mindful of this truth. If we are, then we will find within us a power that outlasts all afflictions and problems, because it is immortal.

3. Before the Beginning

This is a time of uncertainty and confusion, because forces of destiny and opportunity are gathering in the unconscious, almost like thunderclouds on the horizon. You may seem unusually fatigued, or under more stress than normal. These are early warning signals of an impending health problem. Your own powers of analysis, however, are not enough to discern the problem. It is a time for conservative behavior: taking stock, seeking professional help, and trying to identify the problem in its earliest stages. Do not discount symptoms; accept them as clues that help you understand the developing picture and act appropriately.

Physical: Until it is possible to diagnose the problem fully, keep focused in the ongoing useful activities of your daily life. This is a time for pragmatism and the conservation of energy and resources. Cultivate a new capacity for perseverance.

Psychological: New stirrings are arising in consciousness; you need to be aware of them and not be threatened by them. Comfortable beliefs and values may be challenged. Instead of letting them develop into an identity crisis, manage them so that they open the door to new growth and understanding.

THE CHANGING LINES

6: You have been lured away from your intended path; you need to find a way to get back on it again.

5: Take each step with caution and restraint until a clear picture emerges. But don't let caution prevent you from recognizing and seizing opportunities.

4: Humility, and the ability to modify assumptions you have made, will be your most powerful tools in healing this problem.

3: The confusion of this time obscures your sense of direction. Seek guidance.

2: Remain calm; anxiety will only compound the confusion of the time. Be willing to tolerate some interruption in your activities.

1: Be mindful of the limitations of the body. It cannot maintain health if you regularly abuse it. Respect the need to build health.

Unchanging: You have created patterns, habits, or assumptions which are a threat to your well-being. These must be recognized and changed, leading to a new beginning, or serious problems will emerge.

4. Indiscretion

Your health has been impaired by the indiscretions of immaturity—by straining too hard; by indulging in anger, worry, or fear emotionally; by harboring resentments or by ridiculing or criticizing others; or by abusing the innate healthiness of your physical system. Smoking, for instance, would be an indiscretion that harms physical health. The only way to repair your health, once it has been damaged by a repeated indiscretion, is to replace your immature behavior with more mature habits. Since immaturity tends to be self-perpetuating, it would be advisable to seek out the guidance of someone wiser than yourself to help you.

Physical: The physical problem is only a "print out" of an inner pattern of immature emotional or mental behavior. A cancer, for example, may be a sign of a resentment eating away at your character. Allergies can be signs of inner patterns of irritability. To heal this problem, you must eliminate the inner problem.

Psychological: You have been drawn into this situation to gain experience. This is not a test of what you know; it is a test of how you respond to what you do not know. So don't try to solve your problem on your own. Consult expert advice, whether from a doctor, a therapist, a book, or your own Higher Self. Invoke help in learning what you need to know.

THE CHANGING LINES

6: The present conditions are a way of balancing out the indiscretions of the past. Try to understand what they are, and correct these tendencies.
5: By developing a wholesome relationship toward authority, you can achieve the healing you seek.
4: You are allowing fantasies and ambition to destabilize you.
3: Beware of succumbing to temptation.
2: Avoid criticizing others and humanity for their indiscretions. Seek to become a healing force yourself, nonreactive to these issues in mass consciousness.
1: Your real need is for greater self-control and self-discipline.

Unchanging: You have collided head on with a blind spot in your character, habits, or lifestyle. Because you are blind to it, you must seek outside help. Until you do, this blind spot will tend to dominate your whole life and well-being.

5. Patience

New life energy is gathering in your system, but the time is not yet ripe for harnessing and expressing it. The state of your physical and psychological energies is in flux. This is almost like a gestation period, in which new potentials for growth or healing are taking shape. You can do nothing to accelerate this process, but if you act with inspired patience, you can enrich the effectiveness of this time of waiting. Seek to be ready to act creatively or dynamically when the time of waiting has passed.

Physical: This may be a time when any kind of treatment seems to have little effect. But do not underestimate the power of the whole system. Changes are occurring that cannot be measured. Work with affirmations, a positive attitude, and prayer during this time to enrich the treatment being given.

Psychological: The greatest threat to you during this time is your own doubt and feelings of guilt. Conquer these insidious forces within you and establish a basic attitude of confidence and trust. Do not be agitated by your expectations or give in to melancholy; cultivate a serene measure of patience.

THE CHANGING LINES

6: The time to act is now. Even though the odds may seem overwhelming, by taking appropriate action you can achieve your goal.

5: Apparent improvements or gains may only be temporary respites. Use this time to build the momentum of health.

4: You have placed yourself in the eye of the storm. Seek shelter.

3: Worrying about your health and well-being is counterproductive. Focus your attention instead on the healthy parts of your life; bless them.

2: Don't try to force issues at present. Accept yourself as you are.

1: Build trust in the healing mechanism within you.

Unchanging: The situation is beyond your conscious control. The outcome depends on people, conditions, and forces other than yourself. The best way you can help yourself is to dwell in the knowledge that you have within you the capacity to guide and direct the healing process. Ask this healing capacity to help you and cooperate patiently with it, taking the opportunities it presents to you.

6. Stress

Your position resembles that of a volcano that is about to erupt. Strong forces have been bottled up; pressure is building. It will not take much for the forces to erupt. It is therefore important to find a way to discharge these energies without jeopardizing you or anyone else, either physically or psychologically. But just discharging the energy is not enough, for it will quickly build up again. You must also evaluate the basic conflict which is preventing normal action and heal it.

Physical: You are either an "accident waiting to happen" or a prime candidate for an unexpected physical collapse. You are seriously out of harmony with some aspect of your life. Determine what this is, and correct it.

Psychological: Your righteousness or determination is leading you blindly into emotional quicksand. When you start to sink, your first reaction will be to struggle, but the harder you struggle, the deeper you will sink. You need to see that it is your own attitudes that are causing the conflict, and heal them.

THE CHANGING LINES

6: You carry your conflict with you, as a turtle carries his shell. Take care to sow seeds of health and harmony, not additional seeds of conflict.

5: Learning to forgive is your key to restoring health and balance.

4: It is not easy to remained poised in the face of conflict, but a sense of dignity and calmness is your greatest source of strength at this time.

3: You will have to sacrifice righteousness and fanaticism in order to regain your health and stability. Don't miss the opportunity at hand.

2: Don't take on the whole world. Put the emphasis on being helpful and supportive toward others, instead of combative.

1: Your physical health has been weakened by stress and conflict. To restore health, you must withdraw from the source of stress and renew yourself.

Unchanging: You cannot avoid the conflict which is brewing, nor its impact on you physically and psychologically. If you accept the inevitable gracefully, and seek to learn from it, however, you can emerge much stronger than before. If you fight and struggle, as you have in the past, the conflict will defeat you.

7. Gathered Forces

Our health is affected by the health patterns of our community and humanity as a whole. When this hexagram arises, it indicates that your personal health is dependent in part on the health of a larger group to which you belong: your family, your school or workplace, or your community. You will be more than normally vulnerable to contagious diseases, and should take whatever precautions are available to protect yourself. You should likewise make an extra effort to practice good hygiene.

Physical: You are susceptible to "whatever is going around," be it a cold, the flu, or something else. This is not necessarily because you have done anything to deplete your health; it is part of being human. At the same time, you should be careful not to invite vulnerability—for example, by promiscuous behavior.

Psychological: There will be a strong receptivity to the toxins and poisons of mass consciousness, which can work subtly to color your thinking and undermine your sense of individuality. It is important to work daily with the power of your Higher Self to cleanse any such intrusion, especially in your values and principles.

THE CHANGING LINES

6: By learning to identify with the healthy elements in society, you cultivate health in your own consciousness.

5: The wise person sets a good example of health for others to follow, both physically and psychologically.

4: Do not let your well-being be colored by the ups and downs of world opinion. Develop a strong foundation of your own ethics and principles.

3: Society is heading into turmoil. Play your part without identifying with it.

2: Take care not to get bogged down in free-floating moods of depression, fear, or self-pity that are not your own.

1: It might be possible to avoid exposure to contagious illness by rethinking your participation in certain proposed activities. Don't be a recluse, but use caution.

Unchanging: Your receptivity to the conditions of health and illness in humanity, both physically and psychologically, is unusually strong. You may have let your sense of selfhood decline to a dangerously low ebb. Restore your self-esteem and sense of personal worth as quickly as possible.

8. Wholeness

The source of all health and vitality is wholeness. It is ultimately the health of the whole human family that matters the most, not just your individual health. Sometimes we get so preoccupied with our personal problems that we forget the larger context and purpose of health. We get too bogged down in our own selfishness, and this clogs our healing mechanism. If this has occurred, you need to rise up to a new and higher perspective, cultivating a more holistic approach to your health and well-being.

Physical: There is a tendency to overstate your ailments, allowing them to cripple you more than they merit. You need to remember that if your foot hurts, it is unpleasant, but the vast majority of you is healthy, and you ought to act as such. You can control how much health problems affect your capacity to act.

Psychological: The true source of health is the Higher Self. Your healthiness is the measure of how much of the vitality of the Higher Self you express, physically, emotionally, and mentally. Your present problems stem primarily from a lack of the health of the Higher Self.

THE CHANGING LINES

6: Your primary focus should be on healing society as a whole.

5: There are many opportunities for healing at this time, but you must work with a mature level of faith to tap them.

4: The use of meditation to contact the Higher Self is of great value to you.

3: Certain beliefs and convictions undermine your well-being. You need to discover what these are and reform them.

2: The ability to care for others helps activate the healing mechanism within yourself.

1: You have tried too hard to force health onto the physical body. You need more faith and awareness of the healing power of the Higher Self.

Unchanging: You are placing too much emphasis on the needs of the physical body. In order to achieve the level of health you aspire to, you are going to have to learn to draw health from spiritual levels. Your goal should be to cultivate a healthy self-expression, not just the absence of physical problems.

9. Gentleness

There is a desire to be forceful, explosive, and aggressive, but it must be held in check by a constraining influence. If done as a mature expression of self-discipline, no harm will come. But if this force is held in check unnaturally—for instance, by suppressing it—the energies involved will build up and become destructive. The impact they can eventually have on health and psychological stability will be anything but gentle. It can shake you apart. Nonetheless, the only way to heal such problems is to learn true gentleness and restraint.

Physical: The agitated, excitable person needs to learn to control himself and interact gently with life, not forcefully. Resist the temptation to coerce or impose on anyone—yourself as well as everyone else.

Psychological: Human nature is very fragile and easily shattered. If you are in the habit of respecting this delicate balance in others, treating them gently, then life will tend to treat you in kind. But if your behavior toward others resembles the fabled bull in the china shop, you can expect life to be a shattering experience for you as well.

THE CHANGING LINES

6: The path to healing for you lies in small, gradual steps.

5: Act wisely with authority. In the act of coercing others, you damage aspects of your own humanity.

4: It is necessary to uncover repressed patterns to achieve full healing.

3: Be gentle and generous in your thought and speech.

2: Do not take on psychological burdens you cannot carry. Take your work a step at a time, achieving your goals gradually.

1: This is not the time for bold new adventures. It is a time for renewing your deepest values and priorities.

Unchanging: All healing is blocked, until you learn to act gently and with restraint. Your tendency to push ahead regardless of the consequences has exacted its toll. Learn to restrain your impulses and ambitions and act with a higher, nobler motivation.

10. Propriety

Now is not the time to break the rules or experiment in unknown quantities. It is a time that requires proper conduct along set rules. Do not rock the boat, whether it is in the family, at work, or in the community. As long as you play the game with good sportsmanship and by the rules, others will cooperate with you and you will achieve a measure of satisfaction and fulfillment. But if you insist on making up the rules as you go, bending them to suit your own selfishness, you will meet with misfortune. Your health will be jeopardized.

Physical: If you are ill, follow the guidelines and directions of your health professional precisely. Examine the degree to which improper conduct has brought you to this condition.

Psychological: The basis of psychological stability is always a clearly defined sense of self-worth, a strong core of values, and a determination to act with integrity. If you are experiencing emotional uncertainty, it is important to examine its roots and replace them with a strong psychological base of self-esteem.

THE CHANGING LINES

6: Make the examination of your motives, goals, and principles the highest priority for healing.

5: Seek the strength you need to act wisely and properly from your Higher Self.

4: A confession of past sins can clear the way for renewed health.

3: Do not let criticisms by others undermine your sense of self-worth.

2: A guilty conscience will point the way to improper conduct that has led to the problems concerning you.

1: Beware of superficiality, especially in terms of dealing only with the surface implications of symptoms. Look for the causes of your problems.

Unchanging: You have become caught up in the Shallow Life. You need to turn within and rediscover the values, principles, and priorities of your Higher Self. Put them to work in your life.

11. Growth

The efforts of the personality and the plans of the Higher Self are in harmony, producing an unparalleled oppportunity for growth. Whatever your situation, your best way to achieve healing, physically or psychologically, is through an active effort to grow—in character, in ethics, in wisdom, and in love. In addition, your resistance to growth is at low ebb at this time. But this condition will not last forever—your resistance to growth will return eventually. So make sure the efforts to grow that you make at this time are strong enough and sufficiently rooted that they will survive once this ideal time has passed.

Physical: The healing power of the Higher Self is unusually close at hand and available to you. To activate it, however, you must confront the areas of immaturity in your character and strive to reform them, so that you better express the harmony of the Higher Self. This is an ideal time for recuperation.

Psychological: Insights into who you are and what you are meant to be doing will come rapidly. But insights alone do not heal; you must activate the power within the insights and apply it to the work of transforming your character, as needed.

THE CHANGING LINES

6: For you, healing lies in dealing wisely with difficult or restricting conditions.

5: Do not worry. Trust in the healing power of the Higher Self.

4: Hold to the path you have chosen. You are making progress.

3: The mind is clear and lucid. Trust your insights.

2: If you have any tendency to harbor resentments, anger, jealousy, fear, or depression, now is the time to replace them with more wholesome feelings.

1: Do not become preoccupied in your own situation. Find ways to help others grow and heal themselves.

Unchanging: There is a rare opportunity for true healing—the kind of healing that is a permanent enrichment of consciousness. As such, it encompasses much, much more than you alone and your personal needs. Try to become aware of these larger dimensions.

12. Resistance

The power and interests of the personality are so strong they eclipse any real contact with the Higher Self. Resistance to growth and healing is at its highest level; you are slowly starving yourself of the spiritual nourishment you need. No healing or progress can occur at any level until you confront this resistance, determine what it is, and eliminate it. Look to your character. Resistance tends to reside in habits of stubbornness, righteousness, inflexibility, perfectionism, cynicism, grimness, skepticism, atheism, and isolation. You need to break up these patterns of resistance and replant the seed of growth.

Physical: Habits have become rigid, calcified, leading to similar conditions in the physical body. The flexibility and adaptability of the body is decreasing steadily. You need to relax your thinking and attitudes before you become completely trapped in an immobile body.

Psychological: You have become an opponent to growth and change. This is a very unhealthy attitude. You are afraid to take risks or take a chance on life. This fear is rapidly crippling your capacity to act. Your only hope is to reverse these attitudes and engage once again in genuine growth.

THE CHANGING LINES

6: A healing is indicated, *if* you can change the attitudes which primarily constitute your resistance to growth. Seek help from the Higher Self.
5: Yield to the authority of the Higher Self.
4: The resistance you are encountering is not your own, but free-floating resistance from mass consciousness. Beware of pessimism and defeatism.
3: Doubt and skepticism are strangling you like a noose. Don't hang yourself on limited knowledge and false information.
2: Avoid colleagues who are bogged down in resistance. Learn to cooperate with people who are actively growing.
1: You cling too much to the trappings of security. Learn to take risks.

Unchanging: Your resistance is so strong it almost eliminates hope. Until you confront the source of this resistance and take action to reduce it, your potential for healing cannot be activated.

13. Fellowship

The problems that beset you at this time are largely the result of a tendency to isolate yourself from others. Either in practice or in attitude, you are a bit too misanthropic. You need to seek out the company of others and learn to enjoy it for its own sake. Expand your circle of friends and associates; join groups which share your interests. Human beings cannot exist as islands to themselves. Because we are part of a larger system, humanity, we need to participate in the constant circulation of subtle energies that flow from person to person. Good fellowship is a vital part of maintaining health.

Physical: Your intense preoccupation with your own concerns and affairs has damaged your physical health. This damage may include trouble with the circulation, perhaps even anemia. In any event, you need to cultivate a new measure of altruism and interest in the affairs of others in order to restore health.

Psychological: Too much emphasis has been put on the needs of the self. You need to develop a more outgoing, generous mood which seeks to embrace the friendship and help of others, not repel it. There may well be patterns of paranoia or defensiveness which need to be corrected.

THE CHANGING LINES

6: Involvement in helping others produces a level of satisfaction which helps promote overall health.
5: You are trying to exert authority in a situation where you do not have it, causing stress to others and yourself.
4: You need to learn to fulfill duties cheerfully, without resentment.
3: The sense of fatigue that you experience comes from associating with people who drain your energies. If possible, choose other associates.
2: Your high opinion of yourself and low opinion of almost everyone else is destructive both to fellowship and your health.
1: You may find help and assistance by joining a "support group."

Unchanging: You need to make a strong commitment to group life and learn what it means to be an active part of an important group. The group you choose to identify with, however, will either limit you or offer you expanded opportunities. Ideally, the group will be one which serves humanity in some way.

14. Abundance

Whether you recognize it or not, you have been given an abundance of opportunity, potential, and health. If you enjoy good health, express gratitude for this abundance, and make sure that you are investing this blessing well. Use your healthiness to make a contribution through your work, help others less fortunate than you, and inspire others by your example. If you suffer from ill health, you need to ask yourself: how did I squander my abundance of good health? Did I dissipate my energy foolishly? Have I harbored anger, resentments, and envy? How could I have invested my health more wisely?

Physical: A lack of symptoms is not necessarily indicative of good health. The real signs of health in the physical system are 1) a sharp, lucid mind; and 2) a constant revelation of divine life in the way you act. These two elements are the source of abundant life within us.

Psychological: Good health is not a possession any more than wealth is. It is a blessing meant to be used creatively. Use your abundance wisely, by cultivating the expression of generosity, goodwill, kindness, and helpfulness.

THE CHANGING LINES

6: You have come to realize the immense healing power of the Higher Self, perhaps in a dramatic way. Express your gratitude regularly.

5: You have the insight needed to help heal others. Give your support and assistance as opportunity arises.

4: Do not let the good blessings of the past lull you into a false sense of health.

3: It is your responsibility to sustain your state of health. Fulfill it!

2: Even though you may be suffering from ill health, it will be your own innate healthiness that heals you. Let the best within you heal the "less than the best."

1: The good health you have enjoyed may be in jeopardy. Reevaluate your lifestyle.

Unchanging: Abundance builds as we do things properly. When this hexagram is unchanging, you are being tested in your skill and ability to "do things properly." Take extra care to act in harmony with the guidance of the Higher Self.

15. Moderation

There has been a tendency to indulge in excesses or extremes, either physically or psychologically. This has created imbalances which are printing out as illness or limitations in the system. The only way to heal this problem is through moderation. This may be as simple and straightforward as going on a diet to lose weight or as subtle as the need for simplicity and directness in thought and speech. You may also find that your "extreme" has been one of excessive self-control, and your need for moderation lies in loosening the restrictions you have imposed.

Physical: Moderation is not meant to be a way to compensate for extreme behavior; ideally, it is a lifelong practice of sensible health—a sensible diet, moderate exercise, disciplined work habits, good hygiene, a balanced sex life, and no overt abuse of the physical system (smoking, drugs, intoxication).

Psychological: Moderation needs to begin with a healthy sense of self-esteem. Those who are too cocky and smug about talents they do not have, as well as those who dislike and degrade themselves, throw their system out of balance. As the ancients said, "Know thyself."

THE CHANGING LINES

6: Moderation needs to be applied even to spiritual pursuits. Heaven must be blended with earth. Be more balanced.

5: Too much intensity in pursuing goals or expressing authority can undermine your health. Be more balanced.

4: You need to redefine your own self-worth. Be more balanced.

3: Beware the traps of fanaticism and harsh criticism. These tear apart your own system and leave it exposed to ill health. Practice moderation.

2: You tend to indulge too much in emotional reactiveness. Do not let yourself become absorbed in anger, fear, worry, or grief. Practice moderation.

1: Your physical habits have run wild. Practice moderation.

Unchanging: You are walking a thin line. The slightest misstep can cause you to fall. It is very important to approach life at this time with a refined sense of balance in all that you do.

16. Evocation

Your Higher Self has issued a summons—it is calling you to make important changes in your life. It may be pointing to a new direction you need to take, but it could just as easily be reminding you of the need to confront and defeat old patterns of immature behavior that still haunt you. Your need is to listen to this summons and respond as fully as possible to it. You have the capacity to do so; the Higher Self is evoking this capacity and expects you to activate it. If you do, you will soon discover a new measure of harmony in your self-expression. If you do not, the discord of your life will undoubtedly increase.

Physical: The ideal pattern for your health exists in the higher levels of your consciousness, waiting to be precipitated. If you make the changes that have been indicated to you, you can precipitate this ideal pattern and restore healthiness.

Psychological: Important opportunities for your growth and development await you. Shake off any tendency toward passivity you may have and take advantage of these opportunities. Do not be afraid to take reasonable risks. Invoke the help and support you need from your Higher Self to take the next step forward.

THE CHANGING LINES

6: You have heard the summons of the Higher Self and are responding well. Hold to your course with enthusiasm and you will succeed.

5: You are not in touch with the ruling forces of your life. You need to make a major reversal in attitude. Acquire piety, humility, gratitude, and obedience.

4: Your motivations are too heavily governed by selfishness. Learn to think less about yourself and more about others and the world around you.

3: Listen intently to the quiet voice of guidance within you, showing you old patterns to be left behind and new directions to pursue.

2: Embrace changing conditions with enthusiasm. It is time to break out of old ruts.

1: Your physical habits are out of tune with the best within you. Reform them.

Unchanging: You are the only one who can produce improvement in this situation. It is therefore your sole responsibility to initiate change and to act with the measure of enthusiasm required to reach the goal. Invoke the help you need from your Higher Self and proceed with confidence.

17. Adaptability

In Darwin's theory of the survival of the fittest, the fittest are not necessarily the strongest—they are the ones with the greatest potential for adaptability. Life constantly throws us into new situations where we must adapt. We get married, and must adapt our lifestyle; we have children, and must adapt to our new responsibilities; we take on a new job, and must adapt to new expectations; we move to a new city, and must adapt to a different environment. You are undergoing changes requiring adaptation; if you fail to acclimate yourself properly, it could well undermine your physical and psychological health.

Physical: You have put unnecessary demands on the physical body, trying to force it to perform at levels it is not designed to accommodate. As a result, you have "run out of gas" prematurely. You need to adopt a more sensible lifestyle—one that is in harmony with your environment.

Psychological: Any tendency toward stubbornness, rigidity, or bigotry will produce a state of inflexibility that endangers your well-being at this time. Loosen up and learn to adapt to changing times and conditions. Do not take change as a personal threat to you. It is a normal part of life.

THE CHANGING LINES

6: By learning to adapt to a wide variety of circumstances, you eventually learn the art of controlling the events of your life.

5: Trust in your Higher Self to provide for you, and it will.

4: You seem to expect everyone to adapt to your needs. This attitude needs to be reversed. You are the one who needs to adapt to the reality around you.

3: Strong prejudices are preventing you from seeking the kind of assistance that can help you. Don't arbitrarily exclude any source of healing.

2: By accepting the conditions of your life without denial, resentment, or bitterness, you will be able to adapt to them much more quickly and painlessly.

1: The help you need will come through suggestions made by friends or associates. Keep in touch with those who care about you.

Unchanging: You have remained too far apart from the responsibilities of your life. Involve yourself, adapting your attitudes and priorities as necessary. If you remain aloof, your health and psychological stability will suffer.

18. Mending

You have let the physical body or your inner life, or possibly both, fall into a state of disrepair. As a result, you must disrupt the normal flow of your life and focus your attention on mending the damage that has been done. Give yourself the time you need for a full recovery. But for this mending to be successful, you must also use this time to examine the mistakes that led to this state of decay. Repair not just the physical body, but also the emotions, attitudes, habits, and thoughts that injured your health in the first place. If you have injured others, learn the power to clean the slate through sincere apology and compensation.

Physical: The process of mending the body is much like mending clothing. You cannot just put a patch on the tear and expect it to look or perform as new. You must reweave the threads of the fabric so that the original texture and pattern of the cloth is restored. Work from the pattern of your physical health.

Psychological: A breakdown, either in health or in mental stability, is a sign of deeply rooted problems. The time of mending is a time meant to be spent in a careful examination of your lifestyle, to determine what assumptions, attitudes, and characteristics are self-destructive. Once known, eliminate them.

THE CHANGING LINES

6: Even though your problem requires mending, do not become absorbed in your situation. Keep in touch with a higher perspective on life.
5: Do not replace one bad habit with an equally bad one. As you mend your lifestyle, be sure to heed the guidance of the Higher Self.
4: You have let others impose upon you for far too long. Now you are paying the price of ill health. Learn to say no to demands and unreasonable requests.
3: You are in a good position to mend the underlying causes of your problem. Do not worry about what others will think; do what you have to do.
2: Do not blame others for your illness. The patterns that need changing lie entirely within yourself. Accept your illness, then work to mend it.
1: A physical habit (such as smoking) has damaged your health. Eliminate it.

Unchanging: You have made too many false assumptions about life. The need for change has become apparent. Do not waste time pretending otherwise. Face the realities of your life and work to correct the errors you have made.

19. Great Promise

New variables have emerged which bring you great promise, if you respond appropriately. The body's ability to heal itself is at its strongest tide, but you must harness this power by adopting an attitude of expectation, optimism, and joy. Our basic mood has an enormous impact on our healing mechanism. It is up to you to adopt a mood which is in harmony with the enormous potential of this time. Flood yourself with cheerfulness and a delight in living.

Physical: There is an excellent opportunity at hand for self-renewal and healing. This would be an optimum time for initiating new programs of health or hygiene: for going on a diet, for starting an exercise program, and so on.

Psychological: This is a good time to examine your priorities and plant new seed thoughts in your thinking, behavior, and approach to life. These new seed thoughts should reflect the highest and best within you—for example, your determination to act with cheerfulness, optimism, enthusiasm, and goodwill.

THE CHANGING LINES

6: You have an unusual opportunity to help others achieve the healing they need.

5: Take care not to fall into the trap of believing that you have been abandoned by the Higher Self, lest your own foul mood makes this worry come true.

4: Any effort to capitalize on the great promise that lies before you will draw support and guidance from the Higher Self.

3: Carelessness and indolence are your biggest enemies at this time.

2: Long-standing emotional problems, such as grief and depression, can be shaken and overcome, if you make the effort to do so.

1: Be ready to seize opportunities, no matter how unlikely their source.

Unchanging: Your example can serve to inspire others to tap into the great promise of life, and harness it for their own healing. You can be a carrier of health and blessings, rather than a carrier of disease, worry, or fear.

20. Reading the Signs

The state of your health is a message from the Higher Self. To cooperate effectively in the healing process, therefore, you must learn to read and interpret this message. In most cases, the symptoms of your problem can be viewed as signs which help you understand the message. But you can never understand them if you think of them just as symptoms. You must think of them as roadsigns that point toward a greater reality: the archetypal patterns of abstract thought which comprise the real blueprint or pattern for your health.

Physical: Don't make the mistake of thinking that your symptoms are the actual illness. The real illness is the pattern in your subconscious which blocks out the nourishing power of the ideal health known to your Higher Self. If you cannot figure out what these patterns are, consult someone who can help you.

Psychological: You do not achieve mental and emotional health by eliminating your neuroses and psychoses. It is a much more dynamic process, attained by cultivating the outward expression of your Inner Pattern. It is the unblemished expression of joy, wisdom, love, dignity, peace, strength, and abundance.

THE CHANGING LINES

6: You know enough. You need to translate what you know into a healing reality.

5: If you discipline yourself, you can discover the archetypal patterns which, when harnessed, will enable you to restore your health.

4: You can learn much by studying the inner character of others who suffer from the same conditions as you do.

3: Your capacity to read the signs of your condition is limited. To understand your problem, you need to seek expert assistance.

2: Heed your dreams. They reveal to you a great deal about your Inner Pattern of health and how you are distorting it.

1: If you treat only the symptoms of your illness, you will simply perpetuate the problem.

Unchanging: You have never experienced this problem before, so you cannot rely on methods or cures that have worked in the past. You must reach out for new understanding, new guidance, and figure out for yourself how to apply it.

21. The Storm

On hot summer days, thunderheads often form on the horizon. They sweep in and unleash their fury. No one enjoys being caught in such a storm, but after it has passed, the storm usually leaves the air clean and refreshed, the earth nourished, and everything living on it renewed. Stagnant conditions have arisen in your health that can only be cleansed by a major storm. Even though it may not be pleasant to be caught in this storm, if you weather it well, you will emerge from it renewed and stronger.

Physical: Even though the symptoms may not have appeared, some kind of health problem is gathering force just beyond the horizon. You would be well-advised to have a medical check-up. Also examine your thoughts and attitudes, to try to discern where selfishness, bitterness, or rebellion has built to excess.

Psychological: You have been too passive about maintaining your inner health. You have fallen prey to self-delusion, and are no longer able to see clearly how your habits and behavior have harmed your own system. Do not make excuses or rationalizations. Accept the warning and prepare to meet the storm.

THE CHANGING LINES

6: You are blind to the warnings. Unless you open your eyes, the storm will bring chaos.

5: The storm incites you to rebellion. Do not betray your highest ideals.

4: You feel naked and exposed to the storm, forgetting that you have all the protection you need in the love and guidance of the Higher Self.

3: The damage done by the storm is more imagined than real. Do not miss the point by exaggerating pain or suffering.

2: Do not engage in self-pity. That is the kind of response which will perpetuate your problems, leading to yet another outburst.

1: This is only a minor storm. Learn your lesson now and it will not be repeated.

Unchanging: The storm is the creation of your own uncontrolled, immature use of your personal energies. Do not blame anyone else, or your Higher Self. Look to your own rage, depression, grief, or selfishness for the cause of your woe.

22. Materialism

You have fallen into the trap of believing that health is a worthwhile goal in and of itself. This has led you to put far too much importance on the physical body and its capacity to function, forgetting that the body is designed to be a vehicle through which the wholeness of the Higher Self can express itself. In lieu of the health of the Higher Self, you have established an idolatrous worship of the well-energized, symptom-free physical form. This has led you into superficial practices and habits that actually endanger the true health of the form.

Physical: Any good practice taken to an extreme becomes harmful. Do not let your interest in health become an obsession. Healthiness that is paid for with the coin of fanaticism is worse than worthless—it can actually damage your well-being. Obsessions and fanatic practices disrupt the normal flow of vitality.

Psychological: You need to be just as concerned with your spiritual health as you are with your physical well-being. The person who has not cultivated a strong core of principles, ethics, and ideals is just an empty shell. The shell may be elegant, even graceful, but it moves without meaning across the stage of life.

THE CHANGING LINES

6: Having endured difficult conditions in good spirits, you now have the opportunity to experience the true grace of God.

5: Accept the blessings of your life without apology. They are the outer raiments of the Higher Self.

4: Do not betray the guidance of the Higher Self for "conventional wisdom."

3: You are heading for a major disillusionment. Do not be afraid, however, for once you have seen through the illusion, you will understand reality better.

2: You need to rise above the Shallow Life and find the core of meaning that gives purpose to physical activity.

1: Purely physical temptations are hard for you to resist, but your lack of self-control is a great threat to your health.

Unchanging: Having discovered the limitations of materialism, you run the danger of rejecting or neglecting the physical form entirely. This is not a step forward—it is just the reincarnation of strident materialism in a new costume. Instead, you want to strive for a healthy balance between spirit and form.

23. Schism

A split has occurred at inner levels, releasing all kinds of toxins and menaces which threaten your physical well-being. Unless you take action quickly to clean up these poisonous residues, it will soon be too late. Then you will have no choice but to let them be purged through the physical body, at the price of illness and a great deal of discomfort. The schism must also be healed, but even if it were healed today, the healing could not undo the mischief already caused. This must be handled separately.

Physical: Be conservative. Take care of your physical health, and do not expose yourself to unnecessary risk of contagion or infection. Now is a good time to build up your body's immune system, by taking vitamins or supplements.

Psychological: This schism is like a wedge in your consciousness, splitting it into two poles. The cause of it may be a guilty conscience, which knows you have betrayed ethics or values dear to your heart; or it could be an intense disappointment or a sudden shock. It could even be an attack from someone else. In any event, it has resulted in a "stampede" of all the negativity in your subconscious.

THE CHANGING LINES

6: By bridging the schism, you mend a major vulnerability in your character.

5: If you are strong enough and wise enough to call on the Higher Self, you can heal the schism before any real damage occurs.

4: The schism has left you without a way of healing yourself. You must seek professional help.

3: The criticism or anger of others is undermining your emotional stability. Do not let them dominate you.

2: The worst thing you can do is indulge in self-pity. It will drive the wedge in even further.

1: You have hoisted yourself on your own petard. To avoid serious difficulties, you must confront the inconsistencies in your character immediately.

Unchanging: The schism is great; you are going to have to deal with the consequences. Your best hope lies in repenting the behavior that led to the schism and recognizing the damage you have caused. This will cause a sense of shame, but do not dwell extensively in it; replace the shame with a new sense of humility.

24. Renewal

You are emerging out of long period of restriction, illness, or stagnation. It will not be long before you are feeling like your old self once again. But as eager as you may be to put the past behind you, it is important to act conservatively at this time. Rash actions or over-exertion could cause a relapse, so cooperate with the spirit of recovery and renewal. Also, make sure you have learned the lesson of the receding phase of your life, lest you have to go through it once again.

Physical: Take care—your physical vitality is still somewhat erratic, even though it is growing stronger every day. Be sure to rebuild your strength carefully.

Psychological: You are experiencing something of a rebirth in consciousness, but it is still too early to know how you will use it. Will you react by trying to recapture your youth—or will you respond with a greater sense of maturity and a new dedication to making a worthwhile contribution to life?

THE CHANGING LINES

6: The renewal you are experiencing is occurring at subtle, inner levels. It will not be noticeable to others at outer levels.

5: The opportunity of your renewal will not be fully seized unless you act in harmony with your inner spiritual plan.

4: You must leave the past behind and chart an entirely new course. Welcome it with open arms.

3: Set goals for yourself that are realistic and helpful. Don't frustrate yourself as you have in the past.

2: Do not get carried away with the semblance of rapid improvement. Practice humility and gratitude for the blessings that have come to you.

1: Do not try to return to the comfort of what you were before. Life has changed; update yourself. Do not live in the past.

Unchanging: Instead of a genuine renewal, you are merely embarking on a repeated trip on a cycle you have ridden many times before. When are you going to learn the lesson you have so artfully dodged in the past? Until you do, you are doomed to repeat the same cycle, with the same problems, over and over again.

25. Humility

The Higher Self is in control of the situation, and is in the process of taking the steps it deems necessary. As a result, events and conditions may change rapidly, perhaps even in totally unexpected ways. It may seem as though these changes are occurring spontaneously, but you can be sure that every new development or twist of fate has been carefully planned and executed by your own higher intelligence. You can best cooperate by cultivating an attitude of devotion and proper humility toward the Higher Self. Instead of questioning with skepticism and doubt, accept what you do not comprehend with trust and confidence.

Physical: You cannot do anything physically to affect the outcome or change the current direction of your life. Just do not do anything foolish that would interfere with the invisible handiwork of the Higher Self. Hold to your values.

Psychological: Subtle changes are occurring at the deeper levels of your awareness. You are not able to control or direct these changes consciously. The best way to help is to make a daily habit of expressing gratitude and appreciation to the Higher Self for its love, interest, and involvement in your life.

6: You have not cooperated with the Higher Self in a spirit of humility. As a result, events have spun out of control. You are on the verge of chaos.

5: Do not fear unexpected turns of events or view them negatively. There is a larger, benevolent pattern that will reveal itself in time. Have faith.

4: Your vanity and egotism are obstructing forward progress. It will be hard for you, but you need to cultivate a measure of true humility.

3: Any effort to manipulate, scheme, or barter your way toward an improved state will backfire and make the situation worse than ever. Be guileless.

2: Be willing to revise plans of your own to fit into emerging opportunities and conditions. Be flexible.

1: The humble and contrite shall be exalted and blessed.

Unchanging: Be poised. You can be sure that the unexpected will happen. Take it in stride, without being surprised. If you greet the unexpected with humility and cheerfulness, you may be able to glimpse the love and wisdom of the Higher Self at work behind the facade of outer events.

26. Motivating Power

An unusually great measure of power has been building up in your subconscious. It will soon be released, perhaps in an explosive way. Only one question remains: how will it be expressed? In a controlled, creative way? Or in an explosive, destructive fashion? If you are in harmony with the intent of the Higher Self, this potential energy will motivate you to new creative breakthroughs. But if you are engrossed in selfish ambition and the limited dimensions of the personality, this energy will tend to forcefully destroy the structure of your selfishness and limitations. This may well threaten your health and stability at the same time.

Physical: Unless you are able to direct this power into constructive activities, you face the risk of explosive health conditions, such as a stroke or a heart attack. The problem does not lie in stress or bad eating habits. It lies in an inability to handle the tremendous measures of power associated with your responsibilities.

Psychological: You have either taken on levels of responsibility you are not prepared to handle, or you have foolishly repressed strong emotional reactions without neutralizing or transforming them. In any event, the dam is weakening, and may well break soon. You will need professional help to manage the outcome.

THE CHANGING LINES

6: Your creative efforts and diligence are about to pay off. For you, this is the epitome of the expression of good health in this life.

5: Your capacity to motivate yourself and others in harmony with the intent of the Higher Self is unparalleled. Seize the opportunity.

4: Previous failures have led you to the threshold of a successful breakthrough. Do not let the memory of the past hold you back in any way.

3: Common sense and a conservative lifestyle are great assets at present. Avoid wild and excessive indulgences.

2: Personal goals and wishes may seem blocked, as though you have come up against a brick wall. Larger forces supersede them.

1: The tempting voice of physical urges is stronger than ever. Exercise restraint.

Unchanging: Some kind of internal explosion is imminent. If the engine of your creativity is well harnessed, it will power you to accomplishment. If not, it will end up being destructive. Handle this energy with great care and wisdom.

27. Nurturing Love

This hexagram portrays the ideal relationship between the Higher Self and the personality. The Higher Self is saturating its personality with the perfect love, wisdom, and support that it needs to act in life; the personality is poised with devotion, intelligence, and humility to receive this nurturing force and transfer it directly to its talents, skills, and capacities, to be used actively in its daily life. If you receive this hexagram, you need to open yourself more fully to the nurturing love of your Higher Self, and learn to express it yourself through your duties and responsibilities.

Physical: "Man does not live on bread alone, but on every word that comes from the mouth of God." While a sensible diet is of value, you need to realize that true health emanates from the Higher Self. Open yourself to this flow of health.

Psychological: The selfish person cuts himself or herself off from the nurturing love of the Higher Self. Selfishness limits and traps us. You need to learn to express nurturing love to others, through your work, through your responsibilities, and as a citizen. As you give of this love, so shall you receive.

THE CHANGING LINES

6: The demands of others may test you to your limits. They are thinking only of themselves, not of you. But they need your help. Do not be offended.

5: You have not prepared yourself sufficiently for the responsibilities you have taken on. You may feel overburdened. Expand your capacities.

4: You have an excellent opportunity to overcome selfishness by helping and serving others. Learn to care and nurture the best within everyone.

3: Do not expect others to nurture and support you unless you are prepared to do the same for them. You need to change your priorities.

2: As opportunities for new responsibilities emerge, accept them. This is a sign that you are in harmony with the force of nurturing love.

1: If you ground the nurturing love of your Higher Self through productive work and loving responsibilities, you shall receive even greater measures.

Unchanging: You can find all that you need in the nurturing love of the Higher Self. Attune yourself to the perfect balance and health of Life. As you express this balance, you create it within yourself as well.

28. Point of Tension

An unusual number of threads of opportunity are about to intersect, creating what is known esoterically as a "point of tension." For the unprepared person, this point of tension will be interpreted as a crisis. But the enlightened person will view it as a moment of unparalleled opportunity—the kind of opportunity he or she has been anticipating for years. Obviously, our health is more vulnerable during points of tension, but if we are able to see the true dynamics behind the apparent crisis, and remain calm emotionally, the impact on health should be nil. The danger in the situation lies in becoming hysterical.

Physical: Of course, the point of tension may actually be precipitated by a health crisis. In this event, do not lose sight of the true dynamics of the situation—the changes and opportunities that are developing at inner levels. These are the key to resolving the outer, physical problem.

Psychological: Keep in mind that the outer event that triggers this point of tension is relatively unimportant. A true understanding of what is happening can only be discerned by examining the inner forces that are creating this point of tension. This examination will give you the key to the opportunity at hand.

THE CHANGING LINES

6: If necessary, be ready to make a worthwhile sacrifice in order to seize the opportunity at hand. Have no regret for making tough choices.

5: If you understand the reasons behind this point of tension, you will be in a position of true authority as the situation unfolds. Act wisely.

4: You are in danger of taking this crisis too personally. You must remain objective, ignoring insults or criticisms, or you will be distracted and lose the opportunity at hand.

3: The source of greatest strength in a time of crisis is your own well-defined sense of values, ethics, principles, and priorities. Take charge.

2: Keep calm emotionally. Take this point of tension in stride, without reacting.

1: Do not be caught unprepared. It will be necessary to act quickly, perhaps in the midst of chaos, to seize the opportunity at hand. Have courage.

Unchanging: Do not be blinded or awed by the opportunity at hand. Even a momentary hesitation can be costly at this time. The worst thing you can do is nothing at all.

29. Threat

Your health and well-being are threatened at this time, but most likely not by external conditions. The true source of the danger is probably your own emotional habits and characteristics. You have allowed a residue of negative emotional reactiveness to build up in your subconscious, to the point where your sense of emotional tranquillity is very much threatened. You are ready for the proverbial "straw that broke the camel's back." Even minor problems or irritations could trigger a physical or emotional breakdown at this point.

Physical: Your physical health mirrors the health of your emotions. The emergence of problems such as ulcers, allergies, cancers, heart disease, and many other illnesses indicates a corollary condition has existed emotionally for quite some time. This problem must be healed before the physical body can recover.

Psychological: You have indulged in fear, worry, jealousy, depression, grief, or anger for entirely too long. Do not accept the pop sophistry that these are "legitimate feelings." They may be real, but they are not healthy. They are destroying you psychologically and physically. Grow up and learn to transform them.

THE CHANGING LINES

6: By saturating yourself with a deep love for God and His intelligence, you will find that threat and opposition lose their power to harm you.

5: Do not compound your difficulties by responding defensively to the threat at hand. Treat it directly, honestly, and you will triumph.

4: Although others are trying to undermine your stability, you have the strength to defeat this threat, if you rely on the Higher Self.

3: You have let your thinking be taken over by others, either by brainwashing, subliminal suggestions, or intimidation. You must regain control.

2: You are drowning in your own emotional instability. You cannot correct this yourself. Seek professional guidance and support.

1: Consciously or unconsciously, you have accepted evil influences as a normal part of your life. These must be purged before you can achieve health.

Unchanging: Your desires are so uncontrolled and your emotions are so undisciplined that you repeatedly invoke threatening conditions. Wake up and get the message! You need to drastically change your lifestyle and use of the emotions.

30. Addiction

Instead of aligning your personal will and drive to the spiritual will of the Higher Self, you have let it be magnetically attracted to the urges and drives of the body. As a result, you have become highly sensual, needing to gratify the physical senses in order to derive pleasure. This has led to a state where you are actually addicted to whatever it is that stimulates your senses. There is a physical and psychological dependence on some physical stimulant. You need to break this habit and regain control of your physical urges before you can restore health.

Physical: The addiction is not just a psychological attachment; it has become a physical habit that disrupts the normal flow of your physical energies. This will inevitably lead to serious physical problems, unless you regain control and break the addictive habit. You are depriving yourself of the vitality you need.

Psychological: The mind is meant to control the physical form. When an addiction occurs, it indicates that the mind has shirked its responsibility. It has let the physical form take over and make choices. You need to strengthen your self-determination and self-esteem as well as overcome the physical addiction.

THE CHANGING LINES

6: You have learned your lessons well, and now have an ability to heal others with the pure forces and patterns of the Higher Self.

5: Having freed yourself from the sensual life, you have a rare opportunity to work in harmony with the strength of the Higher Self.

4: You need to adopt goals and values that will let you live a life of more fulfillment than just thrill seeking. Redefine why you are here on earth.

3: Accept your problem and learn to grow out of it. Do not blame yourself, nor think of yourself as a victim of society. Don't be a victim; be a survivor!

2: If you had a stronger respect and love for yourself, you never would have let this addiction occur. Take steps to strengthen your self-esteem.

1: The total indulgence of addiction can only be broken by total abstinence.

Unchanging: You are not afflicted by addictions, but you do have important lessons to learn in integrating the lower self with the Higher Self. The lower self still tends to heed its own wishes and urges. It needs to restrain these desires and integrate itself fully with the life of spirit.

31. Magnetism

One of the great laws of life is that "like attracts like." This principle influences our health and well-being in powerful ways, because the physical body itself is highly magnetic, as is our psychological makeup. The very substance of our forms is attracted or repelled by the nature of our attitudes, moods, thoughts, values, and character. If we are noble, generous, wise, and caring, we will magnetically attract substance of a high quality for our physical body, our emotions, and our mind. But if we are selfish, crude, angry, and bigoted, we will magnetically attract a much cruder type of substance. Obviously, the quality of the substance of our bodies has a lot to do with the nature of our health.

Physical: The flow of energy throughout our system is determined in large part magnetically. Your physical problem is caused largely by magnetic impurities. Chiropractic adjustments, acupuncture, and homeopathic remedies can be highly beneficial in producing a cure.

Psychological: Your environment contains magnetic patterns which are causing problems. This could be "free floating" moods at the office or at home, or it could be that you associate with people who are a negative influence on you. Try to discern what these environmental influences are, and remove them, if possible.

THE CHANGING LINES

6: You have a rare opportunity to tap the joy of the Higher Self and integrate it into all that you do. You can acquire great healing power.

5: Your sphere of influence is greater than you realize. Take your responsibility to help and serve seriously.

4: When inspired by archetypal patterns, your thoughts have a magnetic power that can produce the results you envision.

3: You are not a positive influence on the environment around you, including your family. Rein in patterns such as selfishness, greed, etc.

2: Take care not to "go with the flow" of your feelings. They are not aware of the total picture, and can easily draw you into situations you will regret.

1: You are being drawn into an adverse situation. Be cautious; do not tread where you are unsure of the path.

Unchanging: You must accept the conditions and circumstances of your life. If you accept them with bitterness or rebellion, you will do yourself great harm. If you accept them cheerfully and joyfully, you will achieve a power greater than most people ever acquire.

32. Immortality

Obviously, receiving this hexagram does not mean that you will live forever. But there are parts of you that *can* and *will* live forever: the noble qualities of consciousness you have developed. Joy. Wisdom. Love. Peace. To the degree that you have cultivated these and other spiritual ideals, you instill in your character immortal elements. And, if you actively express them, in creativity or service to mankind, then you are infusing your work with immortality as well. The more these elements are part of your life, the more you create a powerful aura of health which not only protects you but also can be a source of healing for others.

Physical: You are confronting the question of your own immortality, either directly or through someone else. This has stirred up worries about health and longevity. Yet the question should not be "How long will I live?" but rather "Am I doing anything in my life worthy of immortality?"

Psychological: Your problems have an immortality you prefer to dispense with: they are negative patterns that keep on repeating themselves and will not go away. You must understand that you cannot escape them; you need to confront them and deal with them honestly. Once resolved, they will not bother you anymore.

THE CHANGING LINES

6: Your wise handling of this situation may permit you to obtain a glimpse of the immortality of the Higher Self.

5: Changes are underway at inner levels that may unsettle you. Reinforce the strength of your values and principles, and hold to them.

4: Your sense of self-worth is excessively identified with the physical body. Try to understand that the true source of your individuality resides in spirit.

3: You worry far too much over factors of life you cannot control. This worry is destroying your health as well as your peace.

2: You cannot lose anything of real value. Do not grieve over apparent losses.

1: Do not try to hold on to situations that have run their course. Accept the inevitable gracefully.

Unchanging: You have a strong ability to endure and persevere, but all too often it is held in focus by a humorless grimness, which is not healthy. You must learn instead to stay on course with cheerfulness and optimism, regardless of the obstacles that try to deflect you.

33. Withdrawal

The situation you are in is undermining your health and stability. If you stay in it any longer, you may reach the point where you cannot recover. It is therefore prudent to withdraw from it, even if it involves risk or sacrifice. This situation is no longer helping you grow and develop—perhaps it never did. You can no longer gain by remaining involved; your best move is to withdraw. Do keep in mind, however, that the withdrawal called for may only be temporary; continue consulting the I Ching for further guidance! Also be sure to define your situation accurately. If the situation referred to is an ongoing argument with your spouse, you are advised to withdraw from the *conflict,* not the *marriage!*

Physical: Some condition in your life is jeopardizing your physical health and well-being. You cannot correct this, so it is necessary to withdraw. If you have asthma, for example, and live in a climate that aggravates it, you would be well-advised to move to an area with a healthier climate.

Psychological: You have chosen a lifestyle that does not fit your temperament, and until you reshape it more realistically, you will be treading on thin ice. Minor adjustments will not be enough; you need to withdraw from the situations which are causing your problems and redefine your approach to living.

THE CHANGING LINES

6: The withdrawal you make will be seen as a wise move, and will actually reinforce your standing and social acceptance.

5: Your ability to make a clean break with the past will generate new opportunities in the future.

4: This is not so much a withdrawal as it is a re-alignment to the guidance and priorities of the Higher Self.

3: You have actually created the situation you must now withdraw from. Learn from the mistakes you have made, so that you do not duplicate them.

2: Examine what led you into this situation in the first place. Do not just withdraw and then jump into an almost identical situation at the first chance.

1: Stubbornness and the refusal to admit that you have made a mistake are compounding your difficulty.

Unchanging: Do not second guess the need to withdraw. You have invested energies in this situation that are being abused or misused. It is not in your interest to allow this to continue.

34. Peak Energy

The energy you need to take charge of your life and energize your best intentions and habits is at a peak. If you are prudent and skillful, you can harness this energy for self-improvement and healing. But this energy can just as easily cause irritation as healing. Therefore, you must be watchful for excitement, overconfidence, nervousness, and even hypomania. Your capacity to worry, resent, and brood will also be heightened. Ambition and enthusiasm might also overpower your normal self-restraint, leading to foolish behavior or speech.

Physical: Your vitality and endurance are high, but beware exhausting yourself needlessly. Too much energy can be too much of a good thing, and may make you prone to congestions of the body, such as headaches, sinus conditions, difficult breathing, or the accumulation of fluids.

Psychological: Too much confidence and enthusiasm can warp your judgment and lead to careless decisions or impulsive behavior. Both feeling and thought can be so stimulated that ordinary fear, anger, or sadness may be overwhelming. Be on guard also against irritability and nervousness.

THE CHANGING LINES

6: Your ambition has exceeded your ability and you may be dangerously overextended. Take time to focus on practical objectives.

5: Beware letting worry or enthusiasm control your behavior. You may be exaggerating issues or trying too hard.

4: This is a time for "working smarter instead of harder." Success depends on skillful execution of wise plans, not strenuous effort.

3: Work quietly and confidently; your own persistent and skillful efforts will produce better results than advertising your problems.

2: Beware overdoing and exhausting yourself just because your enthusiasm is high. Your underlying limits are still there.

1: You need more than ambition and confidence to succeed: skill, courage, and understanding are the real ingredients of achievement.

Unchanging: Overconfidence may cause you to be too attracted to things that are unorthodox and improbable. Be prudent and correct in your analysis and choices.

35. Favorable Change

Conditions now strongly favor healing of the body and personality. Take the initiative—use your imagination and power of suggestion to encourage change in the subconscious and physical form. Act confidently, knowing that you are guided and supported by your Higher Self, its ideals, and its long-term goals. Do not hesitate to seek help from supportive friends and groups. But be aware that you may have to heal relationships, memories, and attitudes as well as a specific physical problem. Be open, honest, and courageous as you take on these issues and heal them.

Physical: Your enlightened action will do much to promote healing. Put to use the good ideas for healing you already know. Your sincere efforts will serve to invoke the power and guidance of your Higher Self.

Psychological: You need to reconcile ambivalence and conflict within your conscience and emotions. Any effort at inner healing will be supported by the healthy elements of your character and your Higher Self.

THE CHANGING LINES

6: You need to reform your values and priorities—or even modify your sense of identity—in order to achieve the healing you seek.
5: If you are certain of your goal, proceed with calm and deliberate effort. Stay the course, regardless of your doubts or enthusiasm.
4: You are basing your thinking on popular beliefs or subconscious wishes or fears. Recheck your goals before you risk your health on these assumptions.
3: You need the help and encouragement of your common sense, conscience, and friends. Do what you need to accommodate them.
2: Sustain your good efforts to heal yourself. While immediate benefits may not be apparent, all conscientious efforts will be rewarded.
1: Subconscious expectations and forces may resist your efforts at healing. Nevertheless, proceed calmly and with faith.

Unchanging: You are in a strong position to be guided by your Higher Self to modify your sense of identity, beliefs, habits, and goals. In this way, you can set the stage for achieving fundamental inner and outer healing.

36. Vulnerability

The forces enveloping you are unfavorable to your health, and your vulnerability to illness is heightened. Without surrendering to distress or fatigue, you need to accept your limitations gracefully. If you press the issue and fight back, you will only exhaust yourself and invite a forceful retaliation by the strong momentum of illness. Practice subtlety, while being totally centered in your awareness of long range needs and goals. Be patient and tolerant, while sustaining a strong faith in your ultimate success.

Physical: Temporarily accept physical limitations and distress, but keep faith that powerful inner forces of healing are at work at unconscious levels. Be steadfast in your determination to endure current problems.

Psychological: Your psychological environment is hostile to you and your capacity to act effectively. Even your subconscious may seem uncooperative. Do not attempt major reforms or self-healing, as you may well provoke additional problems. Accept the fact that some conflict in life is unavoidable.

THE CHANGING LINES

6: Recent difficulties are about to be exhausted by their inherent self-destructive nature. Do not oppose this natural healing momentum.

5: Hold to your values and goals, but be patient with the course of events. You are not yet in a position to fight the problems confronting you. Be patient.

4: You are able to evaluate your situation accurately. It is time to decide whether to continue to fight or withdraw from certain struggles.

3: Recognize how faulty beliefs have contributed to your problems. Begin your reforms now, but at a pace that is healing, not punitive.

2: Look for the hidden message in your suffering. Let it remind you of what must be done to preserve and protect health in the future.

1: Your motives and actions may appear selfish to others. Move cautiously, unless you are prepared to be misunderstood and criticized.

Unchanging: The issues confronting you are part of your destiny or karma and cannot be totally transformed. Assume that your distress and limitations are designed to bring about growth and strengthening of your character.

37. The Loving Parent

True health consists of a harmonious relationship among our inner design for health, our environment, and our conscious thoughts, feelings, and actions. When your conscious beliefs and behavior are not in line with your Higher Self or your environment, you will inevitably experience distress. You need to pay more attention to the cues and signals that will tell you how well you are conforming to these patterns and designs. Fatigue or stress, for example, can be warning signs that you are exceeding your limitations or ignoring basic needs. It is your duty to treat your body and personality as a benevolent parent would care for a child.

Physical: Because you see yourself as someone apart from your body, you have ignored some of its basic needs. It is not a machine to use, but a part of your humanity to cherish and protect. Cultivate a sensible attitude about its care.

Psychological: You have become isolated from others because of a heightened sense of individuality. In assuming more authority than you have earned, you may have also estranged yourself from your conscience, common sense, and inner guidance. You now are experiencing the consequences of this immaturity.

THE CHANGING LINES

6: If you follow your common sense and act responsibly instead of in your self-interest, you will find great success and well-being.

5: Assume the role of loving parent and be your own healer. Treat your subconscious and body with kindness and maturity. You will see favorable results.

4: Examine both the limits and needs of your body and character. Your best approach to healing now will be to attend to these basic factors.

3: Beware of tendencies of self-indulgence as well as expecting too much of yourself. Healing can be found midway between these extremes.

2: Act conservatively and avoid grandiose or impulsive schemes. Attend to your legitimate needs.

1: Clarify your thinking about your responsibility for your own health. Act as a loving parent toward your own body and you will find long-term sacrifice and hardships are more easily endured.

Unchanging: As you grasp your role in creating and sustaining your health, you can identify clearly what you must do now. In fact, you are able to draw great power from fulfilling this responsibility. Your probability for success is good.

38. Discord

You have been inconsistent in your behavior—there are significant contradictions within your attitudes, thoughts, and intentions. The war within yourself is producing a conflict that has not only thwarted healing but has actually contributed to your problem. You need to identify these inner conflicts and take steps to heal them, by establishing consistent and firm intentions and priorities. Do not be too zealous in tackling this problem, however, lest you simply inflame the discord. Work instead from a firm awareness of the larger purpose in your life, modifying your thoughts, feelings, and behavior to conform with it.

Physical: Your problem has been caused or aggravated by the fact that you have been acting against your best interests—or have failed to protect them. Make health your top priority and then exercise some self-discipline and common sense.

Psychological: Your state of mind and environment are not conducive to your well-being. Reevaluate some of your key assumptions and fixed ideas and update them to conform to your current needs. You need to integrate your thoughts and feelings more completely with your values.

THE CHANGING LINES

6: You have strayed from your intended path and now misunderstand the benevolent nature of the forces affecting you. Do not mistake the true message within your adversity.

5: Cynicism or despair may prevent you from recognizing sources of support and help. Learn to accept the assistance of others and life itself.

4: There are others who have suffered or are suffering from problems similar to yours. Seek them out; they can help you now.

3: Align yourself more fully with your inner strengths and the strong people around you so you can endure what you cannot currently change.

2: Intelligent forces around you recognize your needs and will find a way to help you. Be ready to recognize and accept this assistance.

1: You can do little to change your situation. Be patient and view your problem with detachment. The problem will resolve itself if you do not force the issue.

Unchanging: Different elements of your personality and habits are working in contradiction to one another. To resolve this conflict, you must seek to conform to a higher sense of purpose or principle.

39. Barriers & Inhibitions

The problem you are facing is part of your chosen path, and it cannot be avoided or ignored. The outer problem is just a manifestation of an inner conflict and inhibitions in your subconscious. To find relief, it will be necessary to gather strength and wisdom. This can come from authorities you trust as well as from the guidance and healing power of your Higher Self. Avoid the urge to strike out aggressively. This problem requires brilliant strategies, skillful effort, and disciplined self-control. Your perseverance will bring about growth of character and greater self-awareness.

Physical: You need extra help from others or your Higher Self in order to overcome this problem. Seek out guidance and renewed strength. If you follow this path, you will make good progress.

Psychological: Your real struggle originates within yourself. Look within your character for unresolved conflicts or irrational beliefs which have drawn difficult people and thorny problems to you. By replacing these inner patterns, you will heal the outer problems of your lifestyle.

THE CHANGING LINES

6: You cannot succeed merely by being detached and patient. But by following the wisdom of greater people, you can solve the problem.

5: Look to your Higher Self for the strengths and wisdom you need. The healing you seek will come as you learn to cooperate more fully with It.

4: You lack the clarity of thought to see your correct path. Your chances for health will be greatly improved if you seek help from qualified professionals.

3: It is vital to give top priority to building health for yourself, not just struggling against illness and adversity. The problem is within you, not without.

2: You have an unavoidable responsibility to work at healing this problem. The greater issue behind the illness is your need for personal growth.

1: Your current difficulty requires much patience. Wait until you have the strength and understanding to act effectively and correctly.

Unchanging: Your real problem has its origins within your own nature and will therefore follow you everywhere until you conquer it. To solve it now, make a careful evaluation of your beliefs and habits and change them as necessary.

40. Deliverance

You are now in a powerful position to resolve old conflicts and reform unhealthy habits by taking swift and firm action. It may be time to walk away from stagnant or unproductive situations. It is also a good time to drop old resentments, guilt, or discouragement and initiate fresh relationships with others, your work, and your body and subconscious. Recognize the patterns of your life that have died and let them go. If you continue as you have, you will waste time and energy and miss promising opportunities. Give top priority to reorganizing your life and becoming productive again. If you do, fresh vitality will pour into your life.

Physical: Something about your health habits or self-image has been destructive. The situation is obvious; you do not need further analysis or reflection. Instead, you need to take decisive action to reform these problems.

Psychological: You can do much to resolve old conflicts and issues just by letting them go. Worry, grief, guilt, or resentment about being victimized will just prolong your suffering. Drop these feelings and concentrate on re-establishing a healthy, normal lifestyle.

THE CHANGING LINES

6: You can dispose of a major problem by a forceful act of will. If you plan your moves wisely, you can liberate yourself from it completely.

5: The real problem you face is actually within yourself. Take charge of it with all your strength and you should be able to heal it successfully.

4: Some of your relationships with others may be quite unhealthy for you. Reduce or eliminate these contacts if feasible.

3: You may have overextended yourself in some way and are nearing exhaustion. This makes you vulnerable to even greater illness.

2: Certain close ties, or even aspects of your self-image and attitudes, are detrimental to your health. Disavow them now.

1: You have now released yourself from major obstacles and much success lies before you. Take time to reorganize your thinking and plans.

Unchanging: Deep, internal transformations are liberating you from habits or beliefs that have held back your progress. Look for signs indicating the kind of breakthrough that is occurring, then act to integrate this new direction into your values, motives, and priorities. Put this deliverance to work for you!

41. Low Ebb

You are entering a cycle of waning or diminishing force. This decline is part of the natural ebb and flow of life energies. While it will not be permanent, you must be prepared to act conservatively and cautiously in key activities and your approach to living. Your resources, both external and internal, will seem to be limited. Beware of unjustified optimism, extravagances or indulgences of any kind, or any tendency to overwork, worry, or become obsessed. Simplify your life and align yourself with your innermost values and convictions. Accept losses gracefully. Devote yourself to personal growth.

Physical: Your physical vitality is at low ebb. Recognize your limitations and conserve your energies, lest you make yourself vulnerable to greater problems and complications. Discipline your ambitions and activities so that your most urgent needs can be met.

Psychological: Expect a reduction in the intensity of your relationships with others. Accept this change maturely, or you may exhaust yourself and irritate others. Your capacity for creative thinking and even concentration may wane temporarily. Be patient and simplify your life until the cycle reverses itself.

THE CHANGING LINES

6: Spend your time seeking a higher and more inclusive awareness of your purpose and long-range opportunities.

5: This decline is part of your path and perfectly natural. Remain calm and endure this phase gracefully. Benevolent forces are at work in your life.

4: Humility pays off now. This period of low energy will expose your bad habits and weaknesses. Take time to note and correct them.

3: Do not alienate yourself from your inner nature, your past, or your body. It is not their fault your energy level is low. Treat them with respect and care.

2: Be clear about your true needs and honor them. Do not make sacrifices for others or for your career which would weaken you.

1: The time calls for caution and conservative action. Strive for equilibrium in your lifestyle and emotions.

Unchanging: You need to be more realistic than optimistic now. Certain limitations are being forced on you, and you have no choice but to adjust to them. Simplify your activities and regulate your emotions.

42. Enrichment

You have unparalleled opportunities for enriching your character and health. Be certain, however, that your aspirations are noble. The benevolent energy surrounding you can only be used to enrich your life and the lives of your associates. It will not relieve your distress, for example, except as you use it to improve the quality of life around you. Indeed, it may become necessary to sacrifice some cherished beliefs or demands in order to use this energy correctly. If your motives are altruistic and generous, you will have no trouble harnessing the opportunities of this cycle. But if you are self-absorbed and petulant, you will only add to your woes. Express the goodness that you admire in others.

Physical: The time is opportune to work at inner healing. Look for new understanding of the nature of physical health and new insight into the false assumptions that have misled you. Anticipate how you can use greater health to become more productive and useful in life.

Psychological: Your Higher Self is calling you to lift your view of life and self to a more enlightened level. Much healing can occur by learning to treat others with generosity and compassion. Search for insights that are coming to you now. Model your thinking and behavior after the truly wise and kind people you know.

THE CHANGING LINES

6: Even though you can sustain an attitude of goodwill toward all, you lack the power to help anyone other than yourself. Learn to serve.

5: Self-forgiveness, self-respect, and an appreciation for your virtues and healing potential will pay big dividends now.

4: Your common sense and mature values are able to work in harmony with your Higher Self to heal unresolved conflicts and harmful beliefs.

3: Look for the hidden benefit in some loss or humiliation. If you stay centered in your values and do not overreact, this may free you from a hindrance.

2: You are receiving extra vitality at the moment. Conserve it wisely by investing it in a structure of healthy habits and attitudes.

1: You can accomplish much healing by expanding your sense of purpose and improving your attitudes about life and self.

Unchanging: You need to know much more about your situation. Fortunately, you are in a position to obtain this knowledge. But intelligent activity, not analysis, is what you require. Persistent small efforts will lead to success.

43. Determination

You need to commit yourself to the honest truth about yourself and what needs to be done to heal your problem. The essence of your difficulty lies within yourself. You cannot attack it directly without provoking a strong defensive reaction. Beware the possibility that pride and confidence may blind your understanding of the facts. Confession and apologies may be in order. Eliminate from your character and behavior any immature, deceptive, or harmful tendencies. Dedicate yourself to new objectives and values. Use your determination to honor the best and noblest within yourself.

Physical: You have been deceiving yourself about some of your health habits. Beware of rationalizing your indulgence in physical appetites and sensual thrills. Be determined to take charge of your health and discipline yourself better.

Psychological: You have secretly enshrined hidden motives which are contrary to your best interests and conscious values. You protect these "shadow forces" with rationalizations and excuses. You need a strong dose of honesty and objective self-awareness. Do not agonize over the past or berate yourself; instead, focus on the opportunities and strengths you now have.

THE CHANGING LINES

6: Overconfidence and self-deception are your greatest dangers. Focus instead on introspection, humility, and caution.
5: Your problem requires persistent and thorough effort, rather than platitudes and promises. Know your goal and be determined to meet it.
4: You may have become obsessed and blinded by your struggle and are aggravating it in subtle ways. Consider a more skillful approach.
3: You will have to "own" and fight your problem by yourself. You may be engulfed by it for awhile, but this is the correct action to take.
2: Constant vigilance in your effort to control your problem will lead to mastery of it.
1: You need more than determination to succeed. You also require fresh insight, careful planning, and right timing.

Unchanging: Since your problem is within you, success will come only as you act with truth and fairness. Cultivate greater honesty with yourself and others, and look for a new and better way to handle this situation.

44. Impulsiveness

You are being tempted to lower your standards or indulge your whims and wishes impulsively. You are unusually vulnerable to poor judgment and lapses in behavior you will eventually regret. A lapse or failure today may seem insignificant or even quite innocent, but it may well be the doorway to future trouble. The long-term consequences of today's impulsiveness may not be readily discernible to you, but you will have to deal with them anyway. So plan carefully and act conservatively. Build up your values and principles to protect you from silly errors.

Physical: Do not assume that little irregularities of your health are innocent or that you have unlimited vitality to endure extra challenges. Exercise caution and restraint, lest you drop your guard and become vulnerable to unexpected trouble.

Psychological: You are in danger of succumbing to overconfidence or naïveté, which can lead to greater distress than you can imagine. Be cautious about granting small indulgences to yourself or others. Exercise control even over what seems to be a trifling disruption or questionable ethical issue.

6: Something unhealthy has crept into your environment and habits. You need to disavow it quietly, even though others might criticize you for it.

5: Remember your highest principles and purpose and be guided by them. This will link you with the protecting power of your Higher Self.

4: Stay focused in your own values and common sense, but do not neglect friendly contact with your peers, subconscious, or body.

3: Listen to your common sense and conscience; they are sending you warnings about your impulsiveness and temptations.

2: Take control of your bad habits and self-indulgences and reform them. Opportunists are waiting to exploit your weaknesses.

1: The difficulties at hand may grow rapidly, unless you are alert and vigilant now, and take action to thwart them.

Unchanging: You cannot avoid confronting some old weaknesses and temptations which you have not yet brought under control. If you meet them with insight, courage, and skill, you can make substantial progress. Do not be ruled by the impulses of your urges.

45. Harmony

Your health depends upon creating and maintaining a harmonious relationship with your physical and social environment, your unconscious mind, and your Higher Self. Without surrendering your principles, strive to interact with all these elements harmoniously. Keep open lines of communication to all of them, but defer always to the guidance of the one true authority, your Higher Self. To re-establish harmony and health, you may need to sacrifice certain personal habits and assumptions. Where there are problems, determine what is best for all aspects of your character and body, and make this your goal.

Physical: You need to become more sensitive to the unmet needs of your body, the burdens you have placed on it, and the ways you have neglected it. There may also be a hidden, symbolic message in the distress of your body. Treat the body as a partner, rather than a slave.

Psychological: You have become estranged from your social milieu, your subconscious, or your Higher Self. This must be healed. Redirect old habits and traits so that they serve the good of your whole being, not just your feelings or your prejudices. You need to integrate your attitudes, convictions, and behavior.

THE CHANGING LINES

6: By aligning yourself more closely with the Higher Self, you can heal the disharmony between you and other facets of your life.

5: Your power to heal depends on the suitability of your goals and methods, and your ability to harness the body and subconscious cooperatively.

4: You may be too self-absorbed. Become more aware of the life around you. Needed adjustments and healing will then occur naturally.

3: Even if you cannot establish full harmony with others or within yourself, treat your friends—and your own self—with greater affection.

2: Do not resist contact with strange and new elements in your environment or conscience. Something useful may come out of these associations.

1: Isolating yourself, physically or psychologically, is counterproductive. Learn to share your life with others—and with the Higher Self.

Unchanging: Your well-being and health depend on subordinating yourself to the design and plan of the Higher Self. As you respond to this guidance and power, healing will follow.

46. Steady Progress

A constructive momentum is now building. The determination to resolve conflict and heal problems will produce steady progress, if you persist in your efforts. You will note a new measure of harmony, and lines of communication will be improved with all your associates, adversaries as well as friends. There is a stronger rapport with the Higher Self, too. You will be more sensitive to what is correct and helpful to your well-being, and your judgment on health issues will be more clear. It is still necessary, however, to continue practicing your established health regimens. Any break in these routines may halt the steady progress.

Physical: Your past efforts to establish greater health and productivity are now rewarded. If you continue in a similar pattern, your steady progress will also continue. Seize this opportunity to cultivate a healthier attitude toward any illness or disability you may have.

Psychological: You can make steady progress in harmonizing difficult relationships. Those in a position to help you will be more sympathetic to your needs than usual. Make peace with your memories and your conscience. Keep up the momentum of earlier successes.

THE CHANGING LINES

6: Examine your progress, past and present, for important clues which may signal a need to modify your plans or methods.

5: The key to steady progress is persistent, modest effort. Beware of taking recent gains as an excuse to rest and claim victory.

4: Good fortune results from continuing to use the principles and methods that have served you well.

3: Be vigilant lest you take for granted recent progress made toward better health. The battle is not fully won, although success is in sight.

2: Your determination and progress have sown the seeds for continuing success.

1: You have achieved harmony with both inner and outer healing forces, and are responding maturely to their guidance. Do not change this.

Unchanging: Progress comes through the accumulation of many small efforts. Persistence in your work and steady mindfulness of your goals are essential.

47. Confusion

The smooth flow of life has been disrupted by dangerous currents, resulting in chaos and confusion. It is a time of great frustration, for what you say will either be ignored or misinterpreted. People in authority will be unresponsive. Normal avenues of support will be noncommital. Your best hope is to focus on survival and the determination not to get drawn into this confusion. The source of confusion is a chaotic disruption of the emotions. Draw strength and comfort from your values and principles. Do not give in to worry, despair, or self-pity, as these attitudes will heighten your confusion. Activate your courage to be self-reliant.

Physical: Vitality and performance are at low ebb. Conserve what energy you have. Keep faith that your inner life forces will enable you to endure if you remain calm and attend to your basic needs. Your will-to-live can be your strongest medicine.

Psychological: You may have to demonstrate your distress and limitations to others in order to make them known. Do not succumb to fear, grief, or resentment, or you will lose your way. Take care of your own needs, quietly, calmly.

THE CHANGING LINES

6: While the immediate situation may not seem to justify it, a quiet faith in the future will serve you well. The future is favorable.

5: Despite the apparent confusion, do not give up. If you hold your ground, things will improve.

4: Do not be discouraged or feel guilty about the apparent lack of progress. Your sustained commitment to health will be rewarded.

3: Appearances may have deceived you; you may be confused about where to turn for help, or how to measure progress. Be calm until you can discern the correct direction to take.

2: Part of your difficulty stems from being too self-absorbed or inactive. Get your attention off of your own needs and become involved in living.

1: Your greatest danger lies in self-pity and apathy. You have lost sight of your goals and principles and are just drifting in a calmed sea of inertia.

Unchanging: The confusion of the present circumstance is wearing down your reserve of vitality and hope. You are in danger of succumbing to depression. Indeed, you seem to have little control over the situation. Nevertheless, draw strength from your will-to-live and you can put your life in order once more.

48. The Essence

You need to penetrate to the essence of your problem. So far, you have been dealing too much with symptoms and outer appearances. By delving into the inner essence, you tap your basic design for wholeness and health. This gives you insight into the real meaning of your problems and how to cure them. If you look mainly at style, appearance, and visible behavior, you may misjudge the relevance and meaning of the challenge before you. By tapping the essence, on the other hand, you tap the power as well as the wisdom you need to heal yourself.

Physical: You have focused too much on the outer symptoms and distress of your problem. There are inner patterns of conflict, immaturity, and repression which have caused and sustained your difficulty. Look inward for the answers you need.

Psychological: Analyzing your memories will not unlock the complete key to your problem. You must search at inner, subtle levels to find the essence of your situation. If you do, you will discover that you were born with an innate design and plan which provides you with both the wisdom and the power you need.

THE CHANGING LINES

6: You possess much insight into human nature and are in a position to help yourself and others. Contentment is your reward.

5: Your intuitive understanding is heightened and clear, but it will do you little good unless you apply it first to your own healing.

4: You need to rethink and adjust your sense of purpose and plans. Once this internal restructuring is accomplished, your health will improve.

3: Do not let the process of introspection blind you to opportunities to help yourself and others. Put the truth you know to practical use.

2: Modesty or fear inhibits you from using your knowledge and power to help others or yourself. Without use, however, your skills will atrophy.

1: You have become so absorbed in popular theories and disciplines that you are no longer responsive to your Higher Self, which could heal you.

Unchanging: Look within your own nature to find the insights and answers you need to solve your problems. Be sure to consult the wisdom of experts and the power of your own Higher Self for help in healing yourself.

49. Transformation

You and the world around you are in the process of change. Determine the direction this transformation will take and learn to cooperate with it. Appropriate understanding and self-discipline now can prevent destructive and intense inner cleavages from occurring. Examine yourself for habits and beliefs that no longer serve your best interest. Discard unhealthy attitudes. Be clear about your goals. You may need to adjust your whole self-image as well as your role in key relationships. As you bring your life into harmony with the new identity, major transformations can occur more smoothly. Keep active and constructive.

Physical: You are out of harmony with your body and your design for health. This condition has led to the necessity of a transformation which is actually a healing adjustment, if you can accept it. Seek to understand this process and adapt your thinking, attitudes, and behavior to it.

Psychological: Your relationships with others and, perhaps, your own unconscious, is discordant. This is forcing change on you which will be destructive if you fiercely and blindly oppose it. Reduce the stress of this change by seeking a clearer understanding of your values and who you are.

THE CHANGING LINES

6: A new authority is directing your life. Accept this and work out your adjustment to it as wisely as possible.

5: Harness the new life and inspiration available to you wisely and use it to direct the healing changes you need.

4: A major transformation is underway. It will lead to greater health if you are ready to give up old expectations and accept your inner design for wholeness.

3: The process of healing can occur smoothly when you understand the need for change and pace yourself to the natural flow of it.

2: If you honor your responsibility to pursue healing with the utmost courage, skill, and understanding, additional assistance will come to you.

1: Be cautious until you can see clearly what to do and when to act. Impulsiveness is unusually risky.

Unchanging: You are at the mercy of conflict and changes you can neither perceive nor control. Proceed carefully, drawing guidance from your principles and values rather than your feelings or assumptions.

50. Divine Intelligence

Life is pervaded by divine intelligence. Your Higher Self knows exactly what you need for health, and the ideal way to interact with the rest of life. If you proceed on the assumption that you can be guided by this intelligence, you will find that you are. You can tap far more of your inner design for wholeness now than usual. As a result, it is a profound opportunity for healing inner problems such as guilt and for comprehending your life lessons and duties. You can see more clearly your limitations and what the universe will not support in your life. By seeing how all this fits into divine intelligence, you can harness it to heal yourself.

Physical: Work to achieve a greater balance in your lifestyle and to take better care of the needs of your body. The forces of divine intelligence will assist you by energizing your inner potential for health.

Psychological: Clearing up misunderstandings with others can be very healing to you. You can understand more of your role in life now and what you can and cannot do. Learn to rely on the power of universal intelligence to support all sincere requests for guidance and healing.

THE CHANGING LINES

6: Because you are in rapport with your Higher Self, you understand yourself and your role more clearly. This accelerates healing.

5: Work with your inner wisdom and deepen your insights about your place and duty in life. Your intuition can be trusted.

4: It is unwise to proceed until you have clarified your goals, plans, and position in the scheme of things.

3: By underestimating your strengths and abilities, you fail to harness them for effective healing.

2: Align yourself with your inner design and universal order. Others may not understand what you are doing, but your healing potential will increase.

1: Your path to health may lead you toward strange ideas and processes. This may be quite a change from your recent lifestyle, but it is worthwhile.

Unchanging: You are in greater harmony with the forces of health. You have tapped your inner design for wholeness, and it will lead to greater integration and balance in your life.

51. The Unexpected

Powerful forces in your environment or your subconscious may be released suddenly, producing unexpected events and reactions. Your first response may be one of shock or fear. Nevertheless, keep in mind that these changes are directed by benevolent, invisible forces. As a consequence, you should be able to gain insight into your own nature and the healing process if you carefully study these changes. Your faith, strength, and values are being tested. If you respond with maturity and calm dignity, you will pass through this time and acquire new strength of character and renewed physical vitality.

Physical: Unexpected physical problems can develop—a sudden release of energy or a condition of congestion, perhaps even inflammation. Even though these problems are uncomfortable, there is a benevolent intent behind them which will lead to greater health.

Psychological: You may be upset by a storm in your subconscious or the shocking behavior of those close to you. Keep yourself centered in your values and strengths and you will gain in self-mastery, as well as the respect of others.

THE CHANGING LINES

6: Events may seem so chaotic that you cannot act and friends are unable to help. The best plan may be to wait for things to clear.

5: Control your reactions. The instability around you can be managed by staying in harmony with your innermost strengths and values.

4: The unexpected may find you unprepared and uncertain. This will pass, but you will not be able to control events for the moment.

3: You have a duty to modify something in your character or lifestyle. Keep calm, look for meaning, and then, and only then, act.

2: The unexpected may be too powerful to resist. A strategic retreat is the best way to protect your interests and health. Wait for a more favorable time.

1: Great danger may seem to lurk in the very thing you did not expect, but do not be afraid. The problem will eventually clear, leading to success.

Unchanging: You can expect to experience many unexpected upsets until you bring your attitudes and intentions into greater accord with the order and plan of your Higher Self and the universe.

52. Reflection

You need to reflect on the possibility that your own reactions, assumptions, and prejudices have created your distress. Only by calming yourself and going inward will you find the answers. Old fears and resentments, worries about the future, and assorted fantasies may be more of a barrier to good health than you suspect. Meditation and reflection on your inner design for wholeness will help you transcend the noise of your ego and align you with healing insights. Strive for the clarity of mind that can bring health and renewal to the physical body.

Physical: Frustrations and obsessions have caused you a great deal of stress. Seek an inner level of calmness and peace that will neutralize this turmoil and release the inner forces of health. Strive for a new definition of your role in life.

Psychological: Your reactions and fears control you excessively. The more you try to fix things, the worse they will become, until you stop being so reactive. You need to establish a stronger tie with the Higher Self and a fresh understanding of what you need and do not need. Meditation is the key to success.

THE CHANGING LINES

6: By seeking a higher perspective on your situation, the significance of your problem becomes clear, leading to better health.

5: If you center yourself in your Higher Self, you will avoid many mistakes and be better poised to act in harmony with your best interests.

4: It is possible to establish a strong link with your Higher Self, but first you must learn to calm your personality.

3: The tranquillity you need will come by centering in your Higher Self, not by the willful effort to discipline unruly impulses.

2: Your distress is a direct consequence of what you have deliberately been trying to do. Understanding and reform is needed.

1: Recognize the implications of the path you are following. You can save yourself much frustration later if you take wise action now.

Unchanging: You have illusions which prevent you from seeing your situation clearly. Your best hope is to concentrate on being aligned to your inner forces of health—not in analyzing or combatting illness.

53. Evolution

The healing you seek cannot occur rapidly—it must be a slow and traditional process of evolution. Do not be impatient and force the issue; the progress you do make will be stable and permanent. Respect traditions and methods of healing which have proven value. Hold fast to techniques that have worked for you before. Trust in your inner vision of health to impel you and provide the direction you need. Your health problem is part of the larger problem of humanity; as you understand the meaning of this, you will tap the healing power you need.

Physical: Slowly evolving healing forces are at work; seek to nurture this inner healing patiently. See your physical problem in the context of your psychological and social situation, for this will give you insight into what you need to do.

Psychological: The gradual unfoldment of your own wisdom, love, joy, skill, and courage is the best medicine for you. Avoid the lure of a "quick fix"—it will only generate more problems for you to manage. Recognize the role your Higher Self plays in healing you.

THE CHANGING LINES

6: By pursuing intelligent personal growth, you attract the attention and support of the Higher Self, plus its power to heal you.

5: The growth and changes you make in your sense of identity and your self-esteem may draw attack from the dark side of your unconscious. Be prepared.

4: The healing process has stirred up old problems you thought had been healed. Their reprise is only temporary, but proceed with caution.

3: Inner healing operates at a natural pace which cannot be rushed or changed for your convenience. To do so would only bring complications.

2: Inner forces and healing processes are working on your behalf, although the work is not yet complete. Your position is strong.

1: You are experiencing the early stages of the healing process. Your effort to assist it may be inept, but you can learn quickly from your mistakes.

Unchanging: Your path is a slow one, based on evolutionary growth toward greater maturity and health. Learn to support the momentum and direction of this healing change; do not attempt to alter it. Keep to traditional methods.

54. Compliance

Like a child who depends on his or her parents, you need to assume a subordinate role to a "superior person" in order to achieve healing. This could be a medical authority—or it could just as well be your own Higher Self. You are not asked to surrender to this authority, just yield to his or her wisdom and good judgment. Only in this way can you prevent further deterioration in your situation. Instead of trying to remain in control, you need to dedicate your full efforts to holding fast to your values and principles. Rely upon the strength of the Higher Self!

Physical: Keep faith that healing is occurring at invisible levels beyond your control. Let those in authority take charge, as you will only create mischief if you interfere or oppose them. Comply with all their instructions and recommendations. This is no time to view authority antagonistically.

Psychological: Curb your restless will and adopt a posture of true humility toward life, your illness, and your Higher Self. Maintain a quiet, amiable, and compliant attitude. Hold any tendency toward grousing, self-pity, and criticism in check.

THE CHANGING LINES

6: Your personal will is dominated by greater forces. Accept it; be content to be led.

5: Your health is best served by being a loyal subordinate to the Higher Self. Devotion to the ideal is your keynote.

4: Even though you want to take action, restraint and modesty are the best ways to help your cause. A better time for action is coming.

3: Work quietly to preserve your dignity and values, while accepting the reality of those aspects of your life that you cannot control.

2: Only faith and devotion to your ideals can see you through to better times.

1: Trust in the help and protection of powerful friends and your own Higher Self. Work in harmony with their direction.

Unchanging: The healing momentum is stagnant now. The ways you have tried to accelerate healing are not working. It is necessary to begin again, with fresh perspectives and solutions.

55. High Tide

You are experiencing a time of "high tide." The abundance of energy, reward, and opportunity is wonderful, but do not overlook the risks involved. Overconfidence may cause you to commit yourself to obligations you cannot meet, or you may foolishly squander the opportunities at hand. Above all, do not take your health for granted. Build a structure for ongoing health by investing some of the energy of this time in greater self-respect and an appreciation of your strengths and talents. Take time to celebrate the joys of life.

Physical: Do not mistake high vitality and enthusiasm for genuine health. Use this time to take care of your needs and upgrade your long-term health habits. Your power to heal yourself is at a peak, so you can achieve a great deal if you use the power of high tide wisely.

Psychological: Celebrate moments of success and achievement. Express appreciation to those close to you. By sharing your joy and love, you set a tone which will help you in the coming times. Because your power for self-transformation is strong, you will be able to energize your ideals and enrich your self-image.

6: Remember to share your abundance of good-will and joy with others. These treasures come from within and are universal—they have to be shared.

5: Be generous to your adversaries as well as your peers. Flood your dealings with others with good-will and tolerance.

4: Opportunities for greater health are abundant. Be receptive to them and prepare yourself to capitalize on them.

3: As you become more aware of your strengths and abilities, you may also see the shallowness of others more clearly. Be tolerant and forgiving.

2: Don't let your confidence and zeal blind you to limitations set by others, your body, or your subconscious. Temper optimism with pragmatism.

1: Seek the associations and benefits of peers or a network of people who are challenged by the same problems you have.

Unchanging: You may be confused by an abundance of choices to make. It may be more productive to simplify your life by discarding old goals and psychological baggage, rather than complicating it by making new commitments.

56. Movement

You have a strong impulse to move on to new situations and explore new possibilities. Such a move may be very helpful, especially in terms of healing. But make sure you are not motivated by a simple desire for adventure, excitement, or even intellectual stimulation. You need to be guided by a genuine need to grow and expand your awareness. Therefore, proceed—but with caution and humility. Do not make any unwarranted assumptions or righteous demands on life. If you are willing to accept what comes to you gracefully, you will succeed.

Physical: You need to seek new understanding into your problem and how you can support the healing process. It may well be time to learn about mental self-healing, visualization, or innovative approaches to conventional methods. Interest in all kinds of healing will bring you good fortune.

Psychological: You need to examine your experiences, emerging needs, and roles in a whole new light. Revise how you perceive yourself, your relationships, your power, and your future. This will augment your capacity to bring about the healing you need.

THE CHANGING LINES

6: You need to focus on a larger view and sense of purpose. Do not let symptoms distract you.

5: You need a whole new outlook and sense of identity, based on humility and kindness, in order to harness your healing potential.

4: Do not become lost in details and small anxieties. Keep your attention on your principles and long-term goals.

3: In times of change, it is important to maintain good relations with all who are in a position to resent or block you—including your own subconscious.

2: By keeping correct goals and confidence in your own strengths, you will attract the support you need for healing.

1: An excess of humility is self-defeating and delays healing. Convince yourself that your life has value and worth, and then begin again.

Unchanging: You are too attached to old, comfortable ideas and habits. In order to achieve healing, you must discard these old patterns and update your attitudes, values, knowledge, and character.

57. Subtle Influences

Forward progress is best made at this time in subtle, discreet ways—not bold initiatives and aggressive action. The outer moves you make should be small and gentle, linked with the purpose and intent of the subtle influences which control the situation. If you try to plunge ahead forcefully, you will estrange yourself from the forces that are designed to heal you. Put the bulk of your effort into harnessing the inner, subtle forces. In other words, spend your time refining your goals, transforming habits and motives, and renewing your interest in life. As changes occur within you, there will be a corresponding increase in vitality.

Physical: Avoid being impatient or resenting your problem. The work of healing requires you to work indirectly to build up your vitality and general health, through steady daily efforts, rather than attacking the disease. Give your body the chance to do what you cannot.

Psychological: Make friends with your subconscious. Begin by accepting your situation and what has gone before without blame or guilt. Treat your subconscious like a child with hurt feelings, not as a machine or a computer. You need to understand its true needs. Healing must become a mutual endeavor.

THE CHANGING LINES

6: Too many theories and too much analysis will confuse the issue and delay the practical action you need for healing to occur.

5: Persistent, gentle action is the key to healing. Be willing to modify your approach as results occur. Support existing healthy trends in your life.

4: Let your action be persistent and modest, but not aggressive. Skill and courage are needed more than force.

3: Excessive analysis and review are just other forms of procrastination. Work instead with common sense and pragmatism.

2: Forces in your subconscious are sabotaging you. You must discover and conquer these elements before further healing can occur.

1: You need to focus your efforts more intelligently. Many methods can be chosen, but you must choose one and use it persistently in order to be healed.

Unchanging: Act as if you are a respected health professional who has been consulted about changes needed in your body, personality, and lifestyle. This perspective will enable you to understand the issues clearly and work in harmony with your actual situation.

58. Cooperation

The key to health for you lies in greater co-operation, both within yourself and with others. Seek to reduce the incongruency of your motives, thoughts, and behavior. Break down barriers which exist between you and others. Share authority and responsibility freely, while spurning selfishness and self-centeredness. Work to establish a better bond with your own Higher Self. Put your efforts into learning to express more goodwill, cheerfulness, and cooperation as a natural part of your self-expression.

Physical: Your healing efforts are too passive or mechanical. Become more personally involved by identifying your physical needs and what you must do to supply them. Cooperate with those who can help you—including the healing forces within your own nature.

Psychological: You seem to have forgotten that you have something to learn from all experiences and all people. You have become estranged from life. Reexamine your assumptions and motives and revise your attitudes to embody a greater measure of harmony and goodwill, both toward others and yourself.

THE CHANGING LINES

6: You need more mature self-direction. You respond too much to peer pressures, fads, or your own uncontrolled wishes and desires.

5: Rethink your priorities in order to make the right decision about your health. Do not be dazzled by outer appearances. Look for enduring values.

4: Do not procrastinate when confronted with an abundance of good choices. Select on the basis of quality, not your feelings or outer appearances.

3: Healing will be achieved by a commitment to wholeness—not by doing what is expedient or comfortable.

2: Refine and strengthen your values and beliefs. This is your source of stability in times of distress and temptation.

1: Knowing that you are correct in your motives and plans will free you from the need to seek reassurance or advice from others.

Unchanging: Your health depends on your ability to cooperate with others, your Higher Self, and the needs of your personality and body. You are more dependent on their goodwill and assistance than you suspect.

59. Reconnecting

Having spent too much time acting on assumptions and expectations, you are now unable to see what is real and what is just an illusion. As a result, your motives and goals are not in harmony with your body, your best interests, or your Higher Self. It is time to reconnect! To obtain healing, you must define and pursue interests and purposes of mutual benefit to your subconscious, your Higher Self, and your current needs. This will allow you to rise above the pettiness and illusions which have separated you from your inner resources, and set the stage for the healing you need.

Physical: You have neglected the needs of your body by being too driven by your obsessions and expectations. In fact, you may have even poisoned your body with excessive emotional turmoil. Make common sense your counsel, and then adjust your lifestyle to serve the needs of your body.

Psychological: You have become too narrow and defensive in your thinking and attitudes. Healing will require you to revise your sense of purpose and broaden your scope of thinking. Instead of trying to get by with as little as possible in life, seek to fulfill your duties and obligations to their fullest.

THE CHANGING LINES

6: Your expectations and goals need urgent revision. They are taking you into risky areas where you will find little support.

5: You need a new and more holistic vision of your situation—a vision that will evoke interest and cooperation from the mind, the body, and the Higher Self.

4: By breaking down barriers of arrogance and pride, you can summon the ideals and goals which will bring you better health.

3: Reconnect yourself with associates who can help you. Address your collective needs and extend your unqualified cooperation and humility.

2: You must cultivate more openness and trust toward others to solve the problem at hand. Examine your prejudices.

1: Conflict is arising, but can be halted if you do not give in to apathy or arrogance. Reconnect with your goodwill; the situation is worth saving.

Unchanging: You are suffering from blatant self-deception that keeps you from fully understanding your situation. A heavy dose of self-examination will be required to break this pattern. Rely on the advice and counsel of your Higher Self. Listen to your conscience, and take steps to reform!

60. Self-Discipline

If you are serious about improving your health, you will have to start by increasing your self-discipline. You may be drifting in aimless activity or procrastinating; perhaps you have failed to control emotional outbursts or harsh condemnations of others. Whatever the problem, a greater capacity to regulate your behavior is very much needed. Reassess your values and priorities and decide what changes you must make to stop sabotaging your own efforts. Put your energies into productivity and growth—cut out the unnecessary excesses.

Physical: You have been acting in ways that have put too much stress on the body, either ignoring the needs of the body or indulging the body excessively. Now you are paying the price. You need to make some common sense adjustments in your health habits so that equilibrium can be restored.

Psychological: Your attitudes have been imbalanced, leading to extremism. You must understand that both indifference and excitement can harm your health. Both self-pity and anxiety are equally deadly. Avoid the extremes and cultivate a stronger measure of self-discipline, so that you are able to control your feelings.

THE CHANGING LINES

6: Opposing the authority of others or the Higher Self will bring you great distress. Instead of criticizing others, examine what you are doing wrong.
5: You need to accommodate yourself to difficult issues. Neither denial nor anger is productive. Practice greater self-discipline.
4: Try to resolve difficult issues in a harmonious way.
3: You are suffering from your own past indiscretions and excesses of behavior. Make appropriate changes in your lifestyle.
2: You are overly concerned about making mistakes or doing harm. This inhibits you and isolates you from your potential for healing.
1: Gracefully accept the limits of your health and learn to work around them or in spite of them. Do not squander your healing power.

Unchanging: You do not correctly understand your situation. Define your needs and what constitutes true health more carefully. Then work with greater discipline. Your keynotes should be clarity and efficiency.

61. Wisdom

Your health problem cannot be solved by treating it as an alien force to be expelled or destroyed. You must try to see it as a reflection of imperfection in your character or lifestyle. Be willing to embrace this problem and admit that it is yours, so you can recognize its underlying message. Initiate inner dialogs with your Higher Self and your subconscious. Let your imagination be a vehicle for fresh insights. With this new knowledge, you can then act with resolution and clarity to chart a course of action that will truly eliminate the pattern of disease.

Physical: Listen to your body, not as an indulgence, but in order to appreciate the emotional patterns and habits that have made you vulnerable to illness. A wise adjustment in your self-image, attitudes, and habits will set you on the path to enduring health.

Psychological: The dark side of your nature is conveying its message to you through this illness. Stop fighting it long enough to listen to the truth. Healing requires a genuine growth of character, not just a superficial reshuffling of rationalizations and defensiveness.

THE CHANGING LINES

6: You are ready for healing, but the time is not right. Be patient and stay productive in working toward feasible goals, until the proper time arrives.

5: Your strength and virtue are obvious. If your motives and goals are correct, you can accomplish much healing.

4: The meaning of your illness and its cure will be found if you align yourself with the power and purpose of your Higher Self.

3: Do not be misled by your reactions and moods. They are unreliable indicators of your condition or path. Look within for the real answers.

2: When you are attuned to your insights and let them direct you, your actions are automatically a channel for healing and the support of others.

1: Seek your own counsel. Stay centered in your sense of purpose and strengths. Avoid confusion by being detached concerning external influences.

Unchanging: You may be at an impasse until you seek new understanding and a new attitude toward your problem. Take the initiative by temporarily pushing away all assumptions and opening up communications with your Higher Self.

62. Attending to Details

Your health is dependent upon a myriad of small details, any of which could mushroom into a major problem if not kept under control. However, it would not be wise to try to control these details militantly, lest you become unresponsive to the healing forces that can help you. Instead, you need to rely on a thorough and meticulous effort to keep the details of your lifestyle, position, health, relationships, motives, and reactions all in proper order. Use your understanding of your purpose to organize these details and give them a measure of unity. Avoid taking bold actions which would just incite chaos and a lack of order.

Physical: Because of social or career interests, you have neglected the needs of your body. Without indulging it, pay closer attention to its needs and care. Rely on established methods of healing and adopt a traditional regimen for the body's daily care.

Psychological: Do not continue to ignore the many minor irritations of your life. Pride, excessive confidence, and workaholic schedules are dangerous to your well being. Pay attention to the small details of your life. "Steady as she goes" is the keynote of health for you.

THE CHANGING LINES

6: You are striving for too much in areas of quality, quantity, or scheduling. Slow down. A more modest goal and pace will bring health.
5: Too much self-confidence and independence is unwise now. You need help from the Higher Self and experts. Listen to them.
4: Your condition is not strong enough for aggressive healing efforts. Preserve your goals and principles, but work just on maintaining health.
3: You may have been lulled by recent improvements and successes, but do not drop your guard yet. Important vulnerabilities still exist.
2: You will find more security and healing by improving contacts with friends, your Higher Self, and others who can assist you.
1: Avoid the unorthodox. Embrace traditional methods of healing with proven merit. Rebelliousness at this time is dangerous.

Unchanging: Without indulging yourself, attend to your obligations to heal and balance your lifestyle and character. Self-discipline and self-restraint are needed. Let common sense and prudence guide you.

63. The Denouement

Your situation may seem favorable, but there are signs it will not endure. Some decline is bound to occur, but you may be able to control this decline if you begin now to take skillful and firm action. Take little for granted. Stay vigilant and keep up healthy disciplines and activities which have proven of value to you. Be ready to adapt and try new healing methods if necessary. Search for signs of impending decline and take corrective action immediately. Keep a conservative pace and do not overreach yourself with ambitious goals. If you remain prepared, you will be able to keep your vitality and health intact.

Physical: Do not be overconfident about the level of your vitality. Stick with your daily health regimens. Be alert for signs that you may need extra safeguards or precautions for awhile. The key to health lies in prevention.

Psychological: Exercise caution in your affairs and do not overextend yourself. Be especially careful lest others take advantage of your weaknesses. Enjoy the health you have and avoid worry. Moderation, however, will help you preserve the well-being you presently have.

THE CHANGING LINES

6: You have specific responsibilities for your own healing. Fulfill these responsibilities as completely as possible. Passivity is dangerous.

5: A show of arrogance or pride will be risky. It invites your enemies, both from within and without, to sabotage your well-being.

4: Appearances and comfortable feelings can deceive you. Behind the scenes, difficulty is brewing. Exercise care.

3: You need all your expertise and power to achieve and sustain health. Recognize that you may need competent help from others. Progress may be slow.

2: You need to repair and heal your habits and lifestyle. Be honest and forthright about your responsibilities. Act with integrity.

1: The consequences of past activities have caught up with you. Face the truth and base your actions on long-term benefits rather than immediate comfort.

Unchanging: You are temporarily in a safe and secure position. Seek to change little or nothing until conditions change. You can be sure they will.

64. Rebirth

Long-term trends in your state of health are about to reach a climax. This may signal a whole new phase of health and living, or just a new cycle, but in any event you are about to go through a kind of rebirth. Your insights, motives, and goals may change significantly. Because there may be many new and unfamiliar elements to deal with, you should proceed with caution. At the same time, appreciate that you are in an excellent position to make new arrangements and to restructure your mental household, values, and goals. By taking advantage of this, you can contribute to the healing process.

Physical: Because you are nearing the end of a cycle, you have the power to heal and consolidate many things. However, as the new cycle begins, it will expose you to much uncertainty. Despite your current state of health, watch your step.

Psychological: You understand your situation more clearly than ever before. These insights give you the power to work with unusual correctness and effectiveness to reorganize yourself and your affairs. The next step may be a rebirth in your sense of purpose, identity, enthusiasm, peace, or joy.

THE CHANGING LINES

6: Try to conserve some of the vitality and confidence you now have for use at a later time.

5: Correct motives and efforts have led to well-being. Restructure your beliefs and values to preserve this well-being and build on it.

4: If there is confusion, it is because you are undergoing a transformation of basic values and inner ideals. Be firm and forthright.

3: You have reached the limits of what can be done in this cycle. A thorough review of your problem and a fresh start will be needed.

2: If you feel blocked in your quest for healing, be patient. Better times and opportunities are coming. Keep the faith and remain determined.

1: While some reform and healing is needed, do not change anything until you have a better understanding of what needs fixing and how to do it.

Unchanging: As you near the end of this cycle, do not fear change. Fear will rob you of the success and fulfillment you should be enjoying. Be content with what you have achieved, and accept change gracefully.

I CHING ON LINE

This book, *Healing Lines,* is the complete text of the commentary for *I Ching On Line,* a computer program adapting the I Ching to personal computers. At the time this book went to press, the only version of *I Ching On Line* available was for IBM PC's and compatibles. A version for the Macintosh computer is in development.

The cost of the program plus the healing module is $39.95. Other modules, as they are developed will cost $24.95 each. (The program is sold only with the healing module.) Modules being developed include one for business decisions, relationships, and personal growth. Others may be added at a later time.

The program plus all four modules can be ordered as a package for $100, a savings of almost $15. This special rate applies only if the whole set is ordered at one time.

To order the program or any of the modules, send a check or money order to Ariel Press, P.O. Box 249, Canal Winchester, Ohio 43110, or call toll free, 1-800-336-7769 and charge the order to VISA, MasterCard, or American Express. In Ohio, please add 5.5 percent sales tax.

Healing Lines can also be bought and used independently of the computer program.